I0804148

# THE AXE WIELDER'S HANDBOOK

Unless otherwise noted,
all photos in this volume are from the author's personal collection.

Author photo by

Peggy McKenna

Used by permission.

# THE AXE WIELDER'S HANDBOOK

MICHAEL BEAUDRY

Published by
**Horizon Publishers**
A division of Cedar Fort Inc.

Horizon Publishers

www.cedarfort.com

ISBN 0-88290-711-5
v. 2 January 2005

Horizon Publishers' Catalog and Order Number:
C1246

Printed and distributedin
the United States of America by

CEDAR FORT

**& Distributors, Incorporated**

**Address:**
925 North Main Street
Springville, Utah 84663

**Local Phone**: (801) 489-4084
**Toll Free**: 1 (800) SKYBOOK
**FAX**: (800) 489-1097

**E-mail**: skybook@cedarfort.com
**Internet**: http://www.cedarfort.com

# Contents

# INTRODUCTION

*The axe is the healthiest implement that man ever handled, and is especially so for habitual writers and other sedentary workers, whose shoulders it throws back, expanding their chests, and opening their lungs. If every youth . . . , from fifteen to fifty years old, could wield an axe two hours per day, dyspepsia would vanish from the earth, and rheumatism become decidedly scarce. I am a poor chopper, yet the axe is my doctor and delight. Its use gives the mind just enough occupation to prevent its falling into reverie or absorbing trains of thought, while every muscle in the body receives sufficient, yet not exhausting, exercise. I wish all . . . would learn to love the axe.*

—Horace Greeley, *Recollections of a Busy Life,* 1868.

As I stood in the Snow and Nealley Showroom, removing an axe from the rack, feeling the steel, the weight, and smoothness of the handle, my mind turned back to a moment over a quarter century before. Caught up in a "back-to-the-land" fever, in search of tools I would need to build my own home in the wilderness, I purchased my first axe, a Snow and Nealley $2^1/_2$ lb. felling axe. The label declared "Our Best Axe." At the time I owned neither land nor a single tree to even try the axe, but I sensed the axe would play a major role in my life. I have chopped, split, felled, limbed, and notched countless trees with this axe, never regretting the day I purchased it.

My axe collection, also, has grown. I now own several hewing axes, two Hudson Bay pattern axes, three single bit axes, three double bit felling axes, an odd pattern French axe, and two 8 lb. splitting mauls.

Each has its own purpose; some I fancy more than others. A couple were disappointments, too cumbersome to be of any real use. I have become passionate about axes and delight in learning the possibilities latent within each one.

The reason I was in the Snow and Nealley Showroom was because of a particular axe given to me by a friend, Mike Shannon. The axe had a very unusual head and neither of us was certain of its function. The bit was 8" in length, leading us to believe it was a hewing axe, but it was double beveled which was unusual for a hewing axe. The one thing

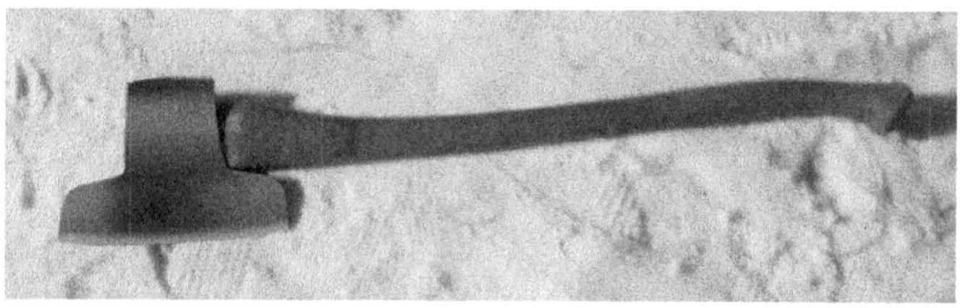

*The mysterious axe: a Webster Pattern Sleeper axe.*

Mike and I were certain of was that the head was clearly stamped "Our Best, Snow and Nealley, Bangor, Maine."

My work regularly takes me by Bangor, so on one of my routine trips I took the axe. I placed the axe upon the counter and asked the salesman if he knew what the axe was called and what its purpose was. He told me he had never seen the axe before. He said to me, "Wait a minute. I'll take it out back; we have a person who has been making axes for close to forty years. He should be able to tell us what it is." A few minutes later he returned, telling me that no one out back had ever seen it before. They were all puzzled by it. By this time the salesperson was as curious about the axe as I was. He said to me, "We have an old 1940's Snow and Nealley catalog, maybe the axe is listed in there." He returned with the catalog, and together we found the axe pattern. The axe was called a "Webster Pattern Sleeper Axe." It said in the catalog that the axe would be fitted with a handle, the length of which was based upon customer request.

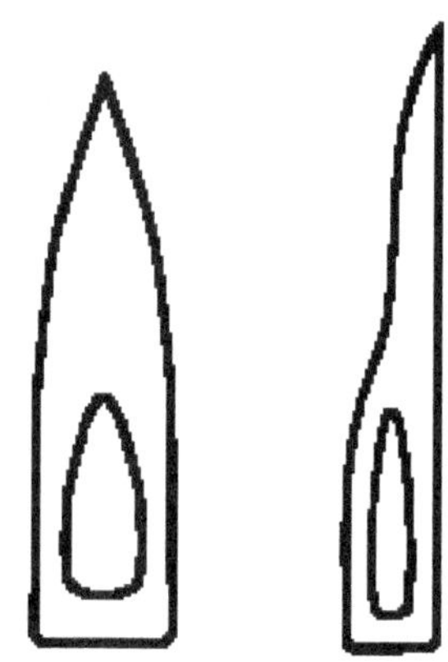

*Double-beveled Felling Axe* *Single-beveled Chisel-faced Hewing Axe*

*Chris Higgins hewing with the Webster Pattern axe.*

A *Sleeper* is a horizontal timber that provides underlying support. An example of a sleeper is a floor joist. Another example of a sleeper is a railroad tie, which serves as the support for the rails. The tool was used for hewing out railroad ties and/or crude floor joist for logging camps. In the 40s wood was still being hauled to rivers, lakes and mills by rails. These woodland locomotives frequently rode on rails supported by softwood ties. The reason the axe was small in size, similar in weight to a felling axe and beveled like a felling axe was because the railroad tie cutter needed a single axe with which he could do all his work. With this axe he could score up the sides of the fallen tree and hew out the railroad tie.[1]

I became equally fascinated with the catalog. In the 1940s Snow and Nealley had an entire catalog to serve the lumbering industry. Snow and Nealley's current listing of axes fits on a simple brochure. Today, Snow and Nealley manufactures the following axes: a hatchet, the 1³/4 lb. Hudson Bay pattern axe (a choice of two different handles, 22¹/2" or 18"), the 2¹/4 lb. felling axe, the 3¹/2 lb. felling axe, the double bit axe, the Pulaski axe, an 8 lb. splitting maul, and a 3 lb. mini-maul for splitting kindling.

Snow and Nealley still produces axes with the same standard of quality they had in the 1940s. Each is drop forged, shaped and ground and tempered by hand. The difference is that, in this mechanized day and age, the mass-market need is no longer there to justify producing a great assortment of axes. Consider the Webster Pattern Sleeper Axe. The logging industry uses roads and trucks to transport logs to the mill. The primary purpose of the Sleeper Axe has vanished and with it any incentive to manufacture the axe.

The Sleeper Axe is not the only axe to be discontinued. Even as late as the 1900s Snow and Nealley manufactured what Cumberland General store claimed was the "last U.S. factory-made Broadaxe available." There were only two left in the showroom. I asked the salesman about the Broadaxe. "We just discontinued them. These are the last two."

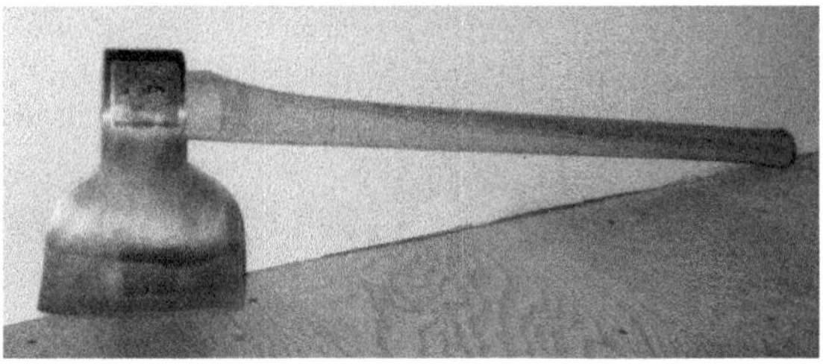

*Snow and Nealley Broad Axe*

I asked about the Froe and the Pickaroon. The answer was the same. Snow and Nealley was discontinuing the tools manufactured for the lumbering trade and was focusing instead upon the needs of the individual with a few acres of woods, a woodstove, or one who likes to kindle a woodfire while camping.

I have been fascinated by the Snow and Nealley Broadaxe for years, but had no real need for one, especially since acquiring a Pennsylvania Pattern Broadaxe that more than meets my needs. I always believed, however, that when I had enough dispensable cash, I would purchase one. I realized that if I wanted one I would have to purchase it then and there, which I did.

It is not merely Snow and Nealley that is phasing out axe varieties. In 1975 Woodcraft Supply sold a felling axe, a German made Broadaxe, two different styles of Kent Hewing Axes, and two different styles of Kent Hewing Hatchets. Only a chisel faced, single-beveled Kent Axe and Hatchet remain. With the availability of axe patterns continuing to disappear, certain human applications are fading from memory, and perhaps will vanish altogether.

One can learn to hew with the Woodcraft hewing axe and become quite proficient, but the tool will never compare to an old Pennsylvania or Canada pattern Broadaxe with an 11 or 12 inch cutting edge. Many of the old Broadaxes (mine included) had a slight ellipse to the bit to keep the corners from cutting into the timber while hewing. The Kent Broadaxe, as with many of the newer Broadaxes manufactured, does not have this feature.

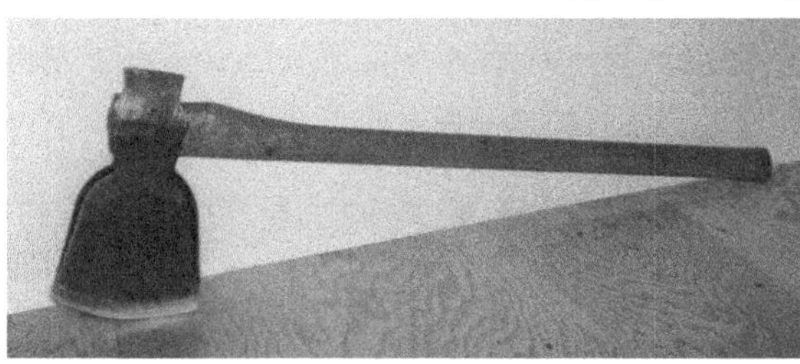

*Woodcraft Supply's Kent Hewing Axe, originally sold double-beveled or single-beveled. Now only sold single-beveled with an offset handle.*

For most Americans, even rural Americans, this is a moot issue. As I visit people, I am always drawn to inspect the quality of their axes. The axes frequently have loose, cracked or broken handles. Nails, instead of wedges, hold the axe in place. The axe is rusted, incredibly dull. Frequently the cutting surface is severely pitted, chipped and peened over, as if the axe were used to crush stone or strike metal. In some cases the poll is mushroomed, or the eye is spread and cracking from years of being driven with a sledge as if the the axe head were a splitting wedge. Axes are used as mattocks, hammers, sheet metal cutters, all destructive practices that eventually render the tool a useless piece of scrap iron.

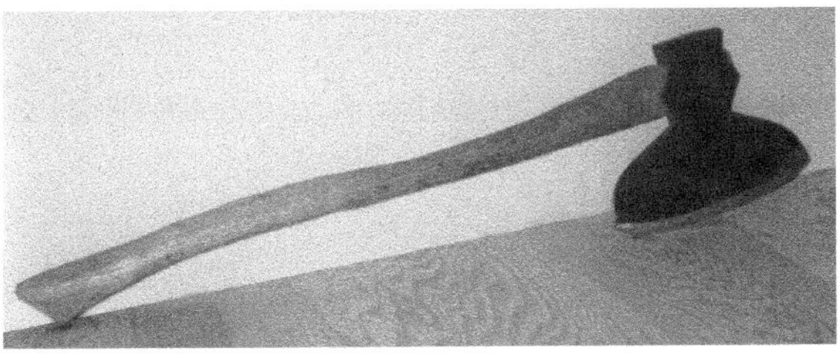

*Pennsylvania Pattern Broadaxe. Offset handle shaped by author from red oak.*

Many of the axes were of poor quality to begin with, purchased cheaply at some large department chain. These axes can be hard to sharpen and/or dull easily. The risk of chipping is increased. Few people know how to properly sharpen an axe, and a dull axe becomes a hazard in itself.

The irony is that the axe is one of humanity's earliest tools, and even as recently as 150 years ago, with this tool alone, a person could build a cabin, clear a farm, enclose the farm with a rail fence, and heat and cook with fuel from his/her own labor. In a sylvan setting, the axe was perhaps the most important tool. When Thoreau borrowed an axe from a neighbor before building his cabin at Walden Pond, the neighbor hesitated while handing it over to Thoreau, stating that it was the "Apple of his eye." It is doubtful Thoreau would even want to borrow a neighbor's axe today considering the condition of so many of the axes I have seen.

I am writing this in praise of the axe. It is my story; more than half my life has been shaped by the axe. But it is a far broader story, one of which I can barely scratch the surface. I wish to share how to use this tool, maintain this tool, and how to develop an environmental ethic living by this tool. The only way to keep this tool from disappearing from human memory is to keep its use and practicality fresh within human consciousness.

# PIONEERING

*. . . it is time to begin to handle the woodsman's axe, to handle it skillfully and to use it as a tool with which to fashion anything from a table to a two-story house.*

—D. C. Beard, *Shelters, Shacks and Shanties,* Shelter Productions.

Twenty-six years ago I surrounded myself with old, traditional hand tools and books on pioneering. Claudette and I were consumed with a dream of building a log cabin. We wanted to live without electricity, cut firewood with axes and crosscuts, and get water with a hand pump. Our idea was to live on the fringe of civilization in as simple and uncomplicated a manner as possible.

We purchased 12 acres in rural Maine and as soon as the papers were signed we were swinging axes, felling trees, peeling logs. The first building put up was a 12 by 20 foot log storage building. The walls were only 3½ feet high with a pole rafter roof. The joints were crudely chopped with the axe; the structure had no floor, mud sills and an elevated loft in back.

The following year with less than $2000, no job, no home and an eight-month-old boy, we moved to our land. The loft in the storage shed became our bedroom, and a $39 sheet steel woodburning stove became

*12' by 20' Storage Cabin*

*Claudette felling a pine*

our cooking and heating appliance. The crude, dark cabin became our home while we built a larger 18 by 22 foot cabin.

*Den and I learning to hew.*

It was an adventure; it felt like true pioneering. I had no skills in building, no carpentry background at all. My only guides were a couple of books. I learned how to hew timbers building that cabin, and all the errors, the crude joinery, the techniques that needed improvement became a part of our home. By winter we were in, the well dug (also by hand) and a bucket with rope was the plumbing. It was uninsulated, drafty, and barely heatable that first winter, but we survived.

The following spring I was asked by a neighbor if I would be interested in

*The early hewing results.*

*Setting the sills for log home.*

*Log home that first winter.*

hand-hewing timbers for a 25' by 36' barn frame. I jumped at the opportunity and commenced work in his woodlot. He dropped several trees and I went about my axe work. Occasionally I used his saw to fell the trees myself. Wherever the trees fell was where I would hew. A few even straddled a creek gully and had to be worked, both scoring and hewing, while standing on the log, the closest footing being the creek eight to ten feet below.

We counted over one hundred and fifty timbers in that barn, four of them twenty-five feet 10" by 10". I used two axes: a felling axe for scoring and a five-pound, double-beveled Hewing Axe for hewing. The axe,

*Bents going up on Barn frame. Timbers hewn by author.*

frequently called a Shipwright's Axe, has a bevel to the cutting surface similar to a felling axe, but the heft of the axe makes it impractical to use as a felling axe.

Working those logs into timbers was a very happy time in my life, breathing the fresh spring air, using the tool I loved best. My skills with

*Placing rafter for barn.*

*Finished Barn Frame*

the axe increased along with my fascination of what these tools were capable of.

Barely a year has passed when I have not hewn timbers. My house sprouted hewn additions and my brother, Den, and I hewed and raised

*Den's house frame. Timbers hewn by Den and me.*

a 24' by 36' house frame for him. I have worked pine, spruce, fir, poplar, hemlock, and oak into timbers. I've hewed for friendship, for wages and for need. Axe work has gone beyond function, it has become passion.

I intended to live without power tools and did in fact—up to about eleven years ago—harvest trees and met my fuel needs with no other tools than an axe and a Swede saw. Time constraints have since made it necessary to use a chain saw.

*Claudette and I on the porch of our home.*

For me, the axe is symbolic of the pioneer spirit: it embodies frugality, simplicity, and independence. I am not a craftsman, nor am I an artisan. That is the beauty of the axe. It is not simply a tool for the exceptional, it is a tool for the common person.

*Our home in winter.*

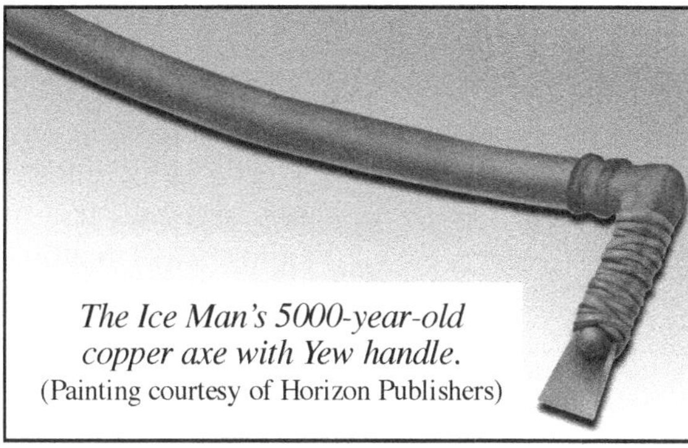

*The Ice Man's 5000-year-old copper axe with Yew handle.*
(Painting courtesy of Horizon Publishers)

# A BRIEF ACCOUNT OF A VERY LONG HISTORY

*So she gave him a great bronze axe that suited his hands; it was sharpened on both sides, and had a beautiful olivewood handle fitted firmly into it . . . . She . . . led the way to the far end of the island, where the largest trees grew—alder, poplar and pine, that reached the sky—very dry and well seasoned, so as to sail light for him in the water . . . . He cut down twenty trees in all . . . squaring them by rule in good workmanlike fashion. Meanwhile Calypso came back with some augers, so he bored holes with them and fitted the timbers together . . .*

—Homer, *The Odyssey,* 720 BC.

The axe is as old as humanity itself. Ancestral man of two million years ago used stones for striking and chopping. Stone hand axes go back 300,000 years, and the handled axes of which our metal ones are a copy date back 10,000 years. The size of the head, its weight, its cutting edge, the manner in which the handle is fitted has remained fluid as new and varied uses have been discovered. And though it is credited with countless deaths through battle and decapitating British nobles and countless fowl, it is in the manipulation of wood that it finds its true value in the human story.

As glaciers retreated and the tundra gave way to temperate forests, a ready source of both heating fuel and building materials became available. With the refinement of the axe—particularly as metallurgy was discovered and improved—the means to harvest this resource was at hand. The evolution of people from hunting and gathering societies to agricultural societies became the key to the axe's refinement, for with agriculture comes a settling-in. Caves and temporary shelters were no longer suitable. Circular huts were expanded into long huts and the means of framing and enclosing these larger spaces became more complex.

The stone axes of the Neolithic Age may have been fine for felling small building poles that could easily be lashed together, but as agriculture became more widespread—increasing the need for more permanent structures—the metal axe became the tool that—in forested lands—made a housing revolution possible. Larger trees could be felled, logs could be hewn square, and timbers joined instead of lashed.

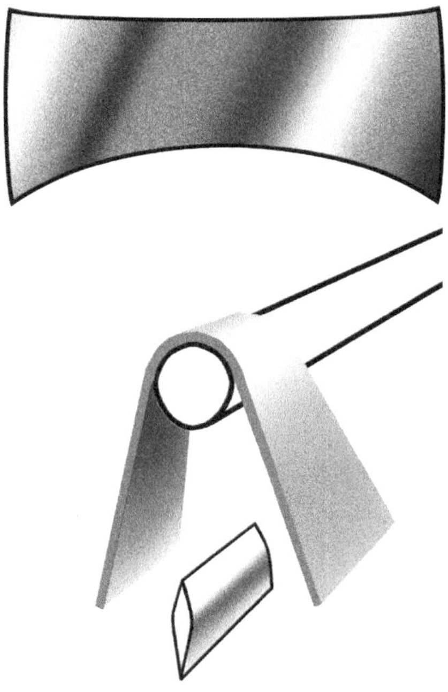

*A strip of iron is heated white-hot and pounded roughly into shape. The axe eye is shaped by wrapping around a rod. A steel bit is inserted.*

The first axes brought to America were polless with gracefully flared blades. So popular was this axe among Native Americans that it soon became the "trade axe." The axe was simple to make and remained little-changed since Roman times. The Romans discovered that a strip of iron could be heated, bent around a rod, a piece of steel inserted for a bit, and the two hammer-welded into an axe.[2]

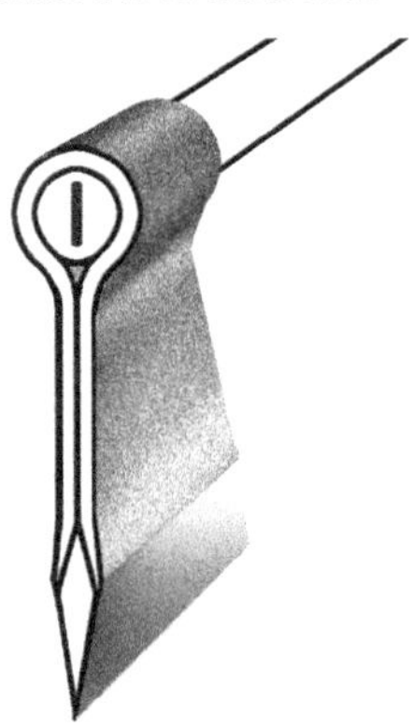

*The iron and steel are hammer-forged, creating the polless axe.*

These axes are still popular in some parts of the world and a few even turn up locally in used tool stores. I recently purchased one (though it does have a slight poll). It had never been handled, and the name Rival was stamped on it. In good light one can clearly see that the bit is of different metal than the rest of the axe head, and that the two metals have been forged together. It is perhaps not the most functional axe in my axe collection,but it is one of the most elegant.

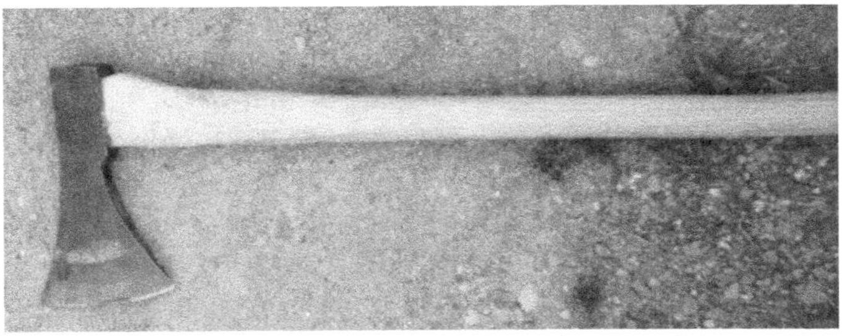

*The author's axe. Note the difference of bit from the rest of the axe head. Handle fashioned by the author out of red oak.*

One American axe that traces its pattern back to the ancient trade axe is the Hudson Bay pattern axe, though even this axe now has a poll.

*Snow and Nealley Hudson Bay Pattern axes*

Though a beautiful and invaluable tool, the colonists, surrounded as they were by virgin timber, were dissatisfied with these polless axes. With all the weight in the long thin blade, it was not balanced and had a tendency to wobble in use. the colonists redesigned the axe. The blade was shortened, a heavy poll added, and the axe itself became more square. By 1740 the new American pattern was by far the most popular in the colonies and has remained so even to this day.

There has been a recent resurgence of interest in early American pioneer tools and implements. This has led to a rise in the demand for trade axes, or tomahawks. Some companies that cater to these audiences have begun manufacturing these tools. If the novelty of such a tool attracts you, it is worth the purchase, but for the same amount of money I can purchase a new $3^1/_2$ pound felling axe or an eight-pound splitting maul.

Generally speaking, commercial axes today are no longer forged of iron and steel. Steel is used throughout. Nor are axes formed by wrapping a piece around a rod and inserting a bit. Today, axes are generally formed by heating a single block of steel in ovens hotter than 1200 degrees C. When the steel block glows a reddish yellow color, the block of steel is pounded roughly into shape with a trip hammer, a belt-driven mechanical device that carries greater force than one could ever create with anvil and hammer. Trip hammers have been used in Maine since as early as the beginning of the 1800s. These hammers were first driven by waterpower and later by steam, petrol or electric power. The steel tool that creates the eye for the handle is driven through the axe while the steel is still glowing and malleable. Once cooled, the axe is ground, reheated, tempered, sharpened and polished.

Americans can take credit for another axe pattern: the double-bit axe. It is not that Americans invented this pattern; ancient Crete had bronze axes identical in design to the American double bit. We can, however, say that Americans reinvented this axe. The axe by design is symmetrical and perfectly balanced. It offers two cutting edges. Should one become dull, the axe need only be rotated 180 degrees and a sharp cutting surface is available for use. In certain circumstances, each bit might be sharpened differently. One bit may be ground with a blunter bit for knocking off dead limbs while the other bit may be ground finer for removing green limbs. By 1840 the double-bit axe had clearly become the preferred tool of lumbermen.

*Double-bit Axe, showing its years of hard use. The handle is of red oak, shaped by the author, and has held up better than the commercial handle the axe was originally fitted with.*

Where forest was thick, it was necessary to thin the trees and to hew felled trees into serviceable beams right there on the spot. The tool for this was the Broadaxe. Broadaxes may have evolved from the Medieval T-Axe.

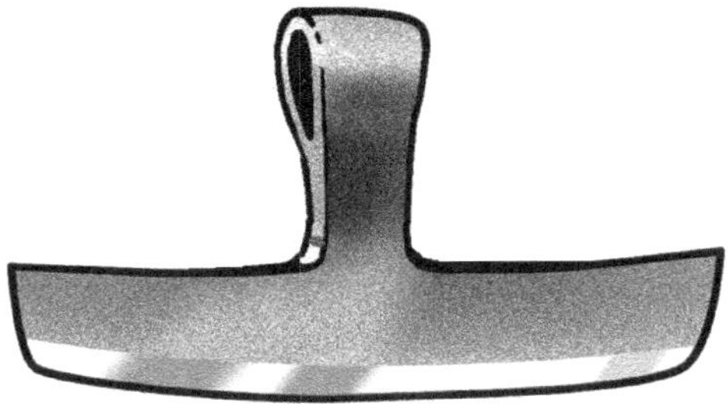

*Medieval T-Axe*

The British developed a symmetrical pattern for their Broadaxe more closely resembling the T-Axe. It is this pattern that evolved into the Pennsylvania, the Yankee and the Canadian patterns. Being symmetrical, the British-American design could be handled either for right or left-handed people.

Woodcraft Supply sells a British pattern Broadaxe. The axe is sold unhandled. One must purchase the offset handle separately. In this way the purchaser can decide which way the bevel is to face. If the person wishes to hew while standing to the right side of the log, the person will keep the flat surface of the axe to the left. If the person wishes to stand to the left of the log, the flat surface is kept to the right.

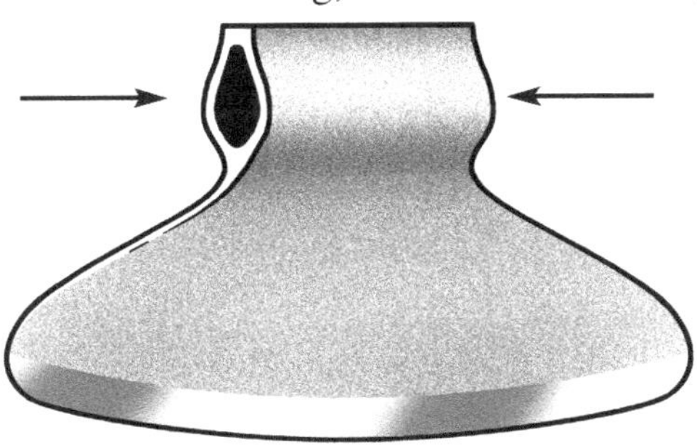

*The basic symmetry of North-American and British Broadaxes enables one to make it either a right-handed axe or a left-handed axe by which direction the handle is inserted.*

The European continent developed a different pattern Broadaxe. They developed the Bearded and Jaw pattern, both frequently—though incorrectly—called the "Goosewing" pattern. This axe lacks the reversible symmetry of British and North American Broadaxes. If one wishes to have a left-handed Broadaxe, it is not simply a matter of inserting the handle from the other side. The axe must be specially made.

To understand why the axe is called a jaw axe or a bearded axe it is necessary to understand the basic anatomy of both the axe and a man's head. When we look at an axe broadside we refer to it as the face, and the axe is described in terms that are descriptive of a human head.

Even the word *poll* is derived from a term used for the human head. *Poll* can loosely be interpreted as *head,* as in *poll tax*. But the actual portion of the head that the word *poll* refers to is the top of the head where the hair grows.[3] To say an axe has a poll is to say it has the portion of

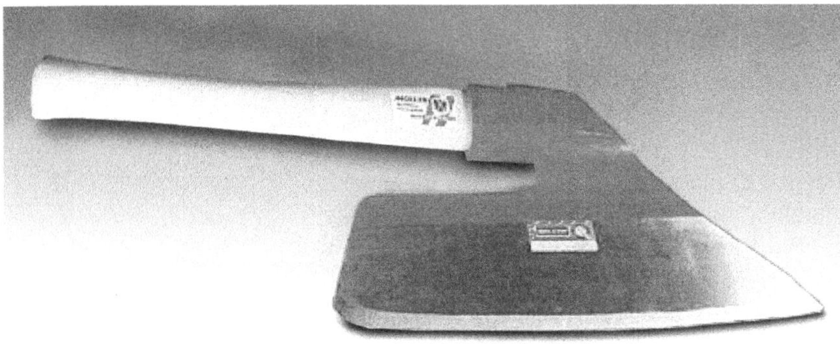

*This German Bearded Broadaxe made by Mueller is also a Jaw Axe.*

the head above the eyes where hair grows (at least for most people). The eye and cheek require no further explanation.

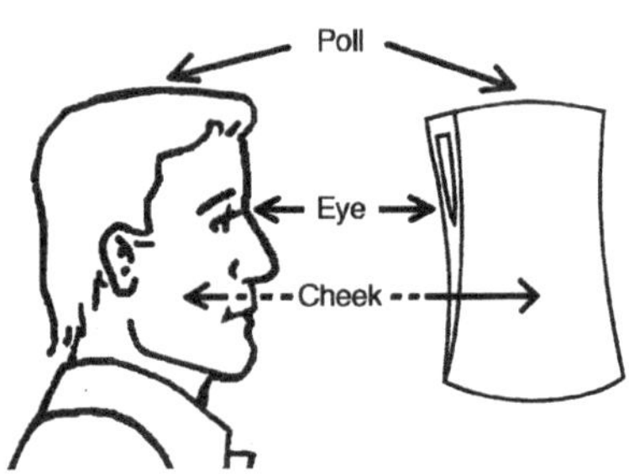


*The **Face** of the Axe*

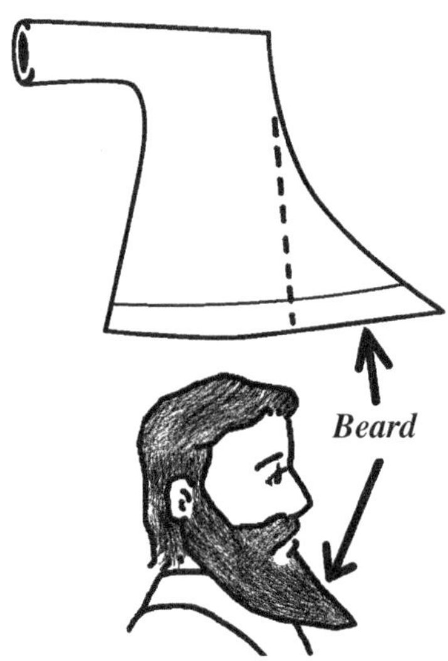


*Comparison of a man's beard to the bearded axe.*

If we consider how a beard grows from a man's face we can easily see what is intended by the term *Bearded axe*. A man's beard protrudes from the front of the face. On the axe this would be away from the handle.

There is an axe pattern that all too frequently is called a Bearded axe, but it is not. The pattern to which I am referring is actually called a *Jaw axe,* because it moves away from the front profile like a person's mandible or jawbone.[4]

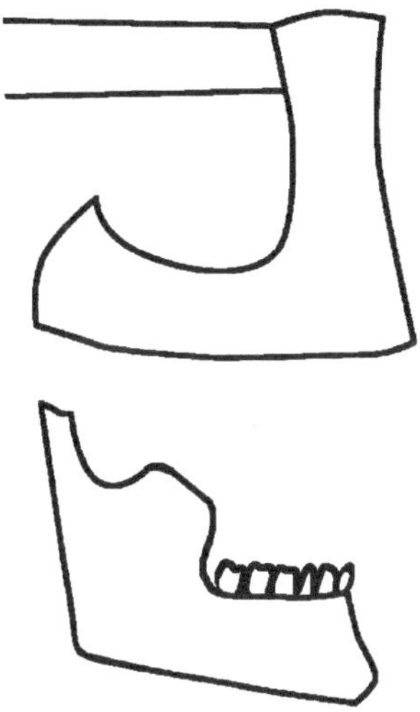

The Jaw Axe extends back toward the handle like a man's jawbone.

Many axes that have the bearded feature frequently have the jaw feature, and, generally, if both features are clearly pronounced, the axe will be called a Bearded axe.

If the jaw is the most prevalent feature, the axe should be called a Jaw axe. Invariably they are misnamed Bearded axes.

I have also heard of Bearded axes being referred to as *Goosewing* axes. The name *Goosewing* for axes came from England where these axes are not even made. An Englishman was basically describing what the bearded axe pattern looked like and the name stuck. With all the other features having names derived from a man's face, it seems unlikely they would use the term *goosewing*.

The poll axe, the double-bit axe and the Broadaxe were incredibly important tools to early America. Ironically, as these tools were evolving into their peak of efficiency, they began their decline. What had been hewn, rived, split or chopped was more and more being sawn, for unlike the axe, the saw adapted well to steam, petrol, and electric innovations—even with computer circuitry. But the axe . . . Alas, the axe is rapidly being forgotten. Few people know what a Broadaxe is or what it is for. The common axe is generally used to split wood in

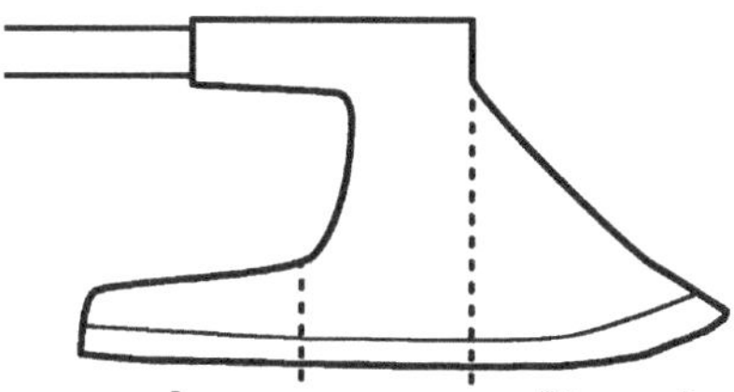


*Though this axe has both features, it is generally referred to as a Bearded axe.*

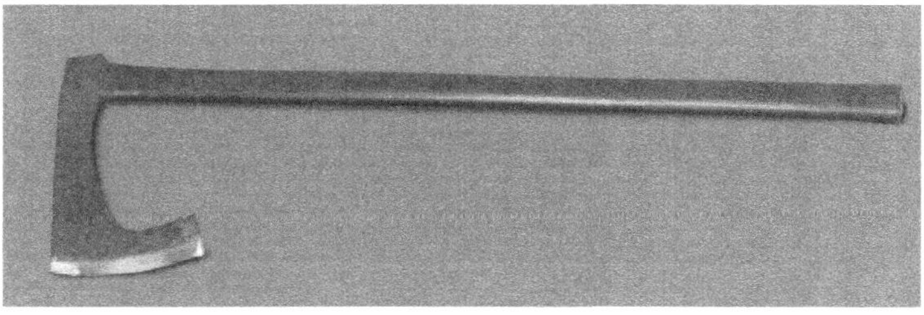

*This axe is advertised as a Viking Bearded Axe, when in fact it is a Jaw Axe. The axe is available at http://www.fantasycutlery.com for $72.*

the following abusive manner: the bit is driven into a bolt, then with a sledge the poll is driven until the bolt splits, widening the eye of the axe until it can no longer hold a handle, or worse, until the eye splits, rendering the axe unrepairable.

Axe varieties are decreasing. Axe manufacturers are disappearing. The lumber industry, which fed the great need for axes in the 1800s, no longer uses them. If you wish for the axe to survive, purchase the tool, learn to use it well, and awaken in yourself a love for this tool, something which happens quite naturally as one learns to use the axe.

*A woodcut appearing in* ***American Pioneer,*** *October 1843.*

# WITH ONLY AN AXE

*The next morning nothing was to be heard but the noise of the axe resounding through the woods. Every one who was expert at that art was gone out to cut down trees to build our friend a house, and before night they had got several of the logs laid out and the house raised several feet.*
—Francis Bailey, F. R. S., *Journal Tour in Unsettled Parts of North America in 1796 and 1797,* Bailey Brothers, London.

When one learns to use an axe to fell trees, buck and split logs, hew and cut notches, one intuitively comes to understand the vital place of the axe in building shelter. Fascination with what the axe is capable of leads one to view shelter in simpler terms. Less of the materials used need be purchased; more and more comes from the work of one's own hands. With but a chain saw, a double-bit axe, a hammer, a few measuring tools and a stand of pine, I could erect the shell of a cabin. The floor joists would be in place, the walls hewn and notched, door jambs in place, window openings framed and rafters set. Give me a froe and the cabin would be roofed. One eventually comes to understand the pioneer's shelter as something that springs up from basically no other material but log, mud and rock, made with few other tools but the axe.

Bradford Angier was an outdoorsman and well-known author, writing about surviving in the wilderness, particularly the wilderness of Northwest Canada, where he and Vena built a cabin and lived for several years. In 1952, he published the book *How to Build Your Home in the Woods,* a book concerned with the construction of inexpensive, rustic log homes. In this book he romantically captures this underlying belief: that a person, equipped with little more than a single-edged axe, could move into the wilderness and construct a serviceable and comfortable home. Angier wrote of a trapper neighbor, Dudley, who in three days working with no more than a single-edged axe, a saw and a few pieces of hardware, built a cabin.

The cabin was only 10' by 12' long with walls that measured thirty inches high. The roof was crudely shaked with poplar shingles split with a limb for a club and the axe for a froe. A few floor boards, called *pun - cheons*, were split out with the axe and poplar wedges along with planks for a door. Angier never alluded that this trapper's cabin was a complex and wonderful example of artistic craftsmanship, but he did allude to something richer. Angier described this man as the happiest man he knew and called him a king living in his spruce castle.[5]

Funk and Wagnall's Encyclopedia affirms the same belief. The log cabin is described as something that a frontiersman could build with but an axe and a knife.[6]

A squatter with little more than an axe and a knife could build a cabin, clear a farm, laying claim to land by some innate right that land belongs to he who works it. When one acquires an axe, one holds, for good or bad, the history of the pioneer spirit. It is easy with axe in hand to romanticize and envision this spirit within oneself. It is Turner's frontier: our classics, our statesman, our philosophers, our legends, our

*This cabin sits in the Lincoln Memorial building in Hodgenville, Kentucky, and represents the birth place of Abe Lincoln. (Library of Congress)*

visions and dreams of freedom, all arising from simple families moving westward into the great wooded wilderness with axes. In the hands of America's "common man" the axe created a farm. And the simple log cabin, sitting in the midst of a stump farm, became the symbol of the honesty of the common man.

This very image, the simple honesty of the cabin dweller, was successfully touted by William Harrison in the 1840s presidential race against the wealthy aristocrat, Martin Van Buren. This historic symbol of honesty remains with us even today, enshrined. And the very values once attributed to the simple frontiersmen have become synonymous with one of America's greatest presidents, Abe Lincoln; the representative log home of his birth remains preserved for all the world to see.

Cabins were generally built through cooperative efforts, like a building bee. Choppers felled the trees and cut them off at proper lengths. One would seek out a proper tree for making boards for the roof. This tree needed to be straight grained and from three to four feet in diameter. The tree was felled and cut into four-foot sections and the sections split, using a froe, into boards half an inch thick. Four corner men were selected. These were generally the best axemen. These men cut the notches as the walls were raised course by course. A rough log cabin

*A Log Raising Bee. Note the four corner men cutting notches.*
*(Woodcut from **The Western Miscellany,** Vol. 1, July, 1848, p. 342.)*

was often built in five or six days. The floor was made of logs split with axes and wedges, and laid with the flat side up. The cabin had a fire-back, or wall of small boulders, built with clay mortar, and a hearth of flat stones. The chimney was round poles plastered with mud.[7]

These log cabins were not the carefully crafted, scribed fit log homes we see today. The notches were kept shallow with large spaces between each course of logs. The spaces were filled with chinks and daubed over with plaster or clay. The chimneys and fireplaces were frequently built of small logs, barely notched and heavily daubed with clay to prevent their catching fire.

A good description of the construction of a log cabin was recorded by Charles Walker in his *History of Athens County, Ohio:*

> The first business of each settler was to make a little clearing and erect a log cabin, which was built of unhewn logs, poles, clapboards, puncheons, and, in those days, wooden pins instead of nails. In its erection, no tools were necessary except an axe, an auger, and, perhaps, a cross-cut saw. Straight trees of the proper size were cut down, and either drawn by a team, or carried with the assistance of neighbors, to the building spot. The logs being cut of proper lengths were notched and laid up somewhat as children build cob houses. . . . The roof was covered with thin splits of oak, something like staves, about four feet long, from four to six inches wide, about one-third of an inch thick. Instead of being nailed, these staves or clapboards were generally confined in their place by heavy timbers, laid at right angles across them, giving the roof a unique and rough appearance. A door-way and windows were made by chopping out logs of proper length and hight [*sic*] before laying them up, so as to make suitable apertures . . . The floors (when any were used) were made of short, thick plank, split from poplar, walnut, or oak. In some cases, the more wealthy settlers had the logs hewed on the inside, and the puncheon floor hewed and planed.[8]

The early settlers could expect to live much of their lives with axes in their hands. In addition to building a cabin, the settlers would have to clear and burn enough land to support crops, grain, hay and pasture for family and livestock. Prior to moving west of the Mississippi, the land upon which the settlers built was covered, for the most part, with forest that had never been heavily harvested by people. Much of this land was covered with, by our standards, uncommonly heavy growth of timber. With little or no means of getting this wood to a mill, much of it was felled and burned. Sometimes the early settlers girded large trees by chopping out large chips, through the bark, deep into the sapwood, all the way around the tree, preventing moisture and mineral nutrients from rising up the tree trunk. The girded trees were left to die and fall as they decayed. The smaller trees were cut and burned. This practice, however, was not the common method. It proved dangerous to people and livestock as the decaying trees could drop large rotting limbs without warning.[9]

The method generally adopted by persons who felled trees by the acre was as follows:

> The chopper observed the direction in which they leaned and could be made to fall advantageously. He selected a range, at the head of which was a large tree, a little elevated, with branching, heavy limbs to be used as a "driver." The trees were cut about half way through, and the chips so taken out, that, when the trees fell, the tops would lie in an angular direction towards each other along the whole range. The "driver," being then cut through, fell upon the next trees, and these in turn upon the next, and so on till the whole range came down with a tremendous crash. Thus half the labor was saved, and the tops were brought together in a favorable position to be burnt.[10]

Though I have felled many trees, I have never attempted to clear heavily forested land. I generally do not fell the largest trees on my property. However, when I fell large trees, I experience a certain level of nervousness while cutting the wedge and felling cut. And there is a strange sort of exhilaration I experience as the tree leans, groans, cracks, and crashes through limbs, thundering to the ground. The exhilaration is like standing out in a hurricane to experience the full fury of uncontrollable wind. The suddenly released power sends a rush through my whole body as I scramble to be clear of the butt's kickback. Even with that experience, I cannot imagine the thunderous crashing that the above "domino" method would cause.

I have felled enough trees to know that such a method probably did not go off without a hitch. To fell one tree toward another is a good way to get trees hopelessly hung up. There is perhaps nothing more dangerous than trying to drop a leaning tree by felling the tree that the leaner is tangled in. Once the tree being felled begins to move downward, the feller has not merely one tree to get clear of, but has the leaner, which now is falling directly onto him. Most people living in rural wooded areas have stories about the neighbor or friend who died or was disabled while trying to free a leaner.

With the amount of tree felling that was necessary, it was inevitable that serious accidents would occur. One of the earliest settlers of Palermo, Maine, John Marden, left this account:

> My father's name was Stephen Marden. . . . When I was 2 years and 4 months old my father died being killed by the fall of a tree in the town of New Hampton, in the county of Strafford, N. H., on the 19 day of June 1781. . . . I came to Sheepscot Great Pond Settlement, now Palermo, 1793 with one of my brothers and sisters. . . . January 22, 1805 about two o'clock in the day I was wounded by the fall of a tree while at work for my brother Stephen on Marden Hill. . . . [T]he tree fell and caught me by the leg and held me until [Stephen] returned. . . . On the 3 day of February I had my left leg amputated above the knee.[11]

In John Marden's story we see the untimely tragedy the axe could bring into a family's life.

There was, noted by many, a particular order to the pattern of settlement. It was described as a natural progression as wilderness became farmland. This progression was well expressed by Rev. John Peck in 1836, and became immortalized when Frederick Jackson Turner included it in his thesis, *The Significance of the Frontier in American History.* Peck described settlement as a series of distinct waves. First came the pioneer, of whom Peck wrote, "It is quite immaterial whether he ever becomes the owner of the soil. He is the occupant for the time being, pays no rent, and feels as independent as the 'lord of the manor.'"[12] The second "wave" of settlers purchase the land, put up more substantial housing than the rough log cabin, and "exhibit the picture and form of plain, frugal, civilized life."[13] The third wave are the men of capital and enterprise that transform the village into the spacious town with colleges, churches, and all the luxuries and refinements of civilized society.

When it comes to axe wielding settlers, we are concerned with the first two waves of settlers. Many of the first wave become the second wave. Peck wrote of the settlers, as Cole painted them, with a Romantic eye, a movement sweeping through the early Republic. But, nonetheless, there is a great deal of truth in what he wrote. If we look at Sibley's *History of Union,* we see clear examples of this transition from wilderness and crude cabins to open land and "more substantial housing."

The first log cabin built in what was to become Union, Maine was built by Bill Packard in 1775. It was an 18' by 20' cabin with a cat and clay chimney and a stone fire-back. Packard and two Butler brothers worked daily, chopping trees and clearing land for grain cultivation. In 1777, Philip Robbins, having purchased the property, moved into the Packard cabin with his family and his son David's family. Fourteen in all lived in the small cabin for four years. Robbins focused on hewing timbers for a barn frame, which he raised by the fall of 1777. Robbins also erected a hewn timber house. The timbers were squared, 12" by 12" spruce beams. The corners were locked with dovetail joints.

In 1779, three unmarried men, Adams, Hawes and Ware, purchased a large tract of land on the northwest side of Round Pond. The three put together a log cabin they aptly called the "Royal Mess." They divided the land into three farms. Together they lived in the log house until sufficient land was cleared for each to farm. When Mr. Hawes prepared to move out of the "Royal Mess," he decided to build a log house a little more stylish than others on the plantation. The house was shingled with shakes split by Hawes, himself. Sawn boards were used for the floor and bricks fired for the chimney. The house had glass windows instead of oiled paper, and the logs were hewn smooth on the inside and out.

We see with Hawes and Robbins a refinement of axemanship in their homes. The new homes are of hewn timber. In Hawes' case, however, we see a moving away from the axe with sawn floor incorporated into the house. Eventually hewn post and truss frames replaced hewn log homes. The houses were finished with sawn boards, shingles and clapboards and, on the inside, lath and plaster. With time, even the hewn post and truss frame was replaced with sawn materials.[14]

But it is in this transition phase, when sufficient land is cleared and the temporary cabin can be abandoned for a more refined log home, that true craftsmanship appears.

Even after the Eastern woodlands had been settled and pioneers had moved across the Mississippi and onto the tree-barren plains, the story was kept alive by axe-wielding loggers in the camps of the great north woods.

Thoreau, in his 1846 trip to the Maine Woods, described the houses and camps of the loggers as "very proper houses, the stems of trees collected together and piled up around a man to keep out wind and rain—made of living green logs, hanging with moss and lichen, and with the curls and fringes of yellow birch, and dripping resin, fresh and moist, and redolent of swampy odors, with that sort of vigor and perrenialness

A more refined appearance: hewn and dovetail notched.

even about them that toadstools suggest."[15] The unpeeled logs and the dampness suggest the immediacy with which these cabins were built.

Thoreau found these camps to be about 15' by 20'. He described one:

> [B]uilt of logs,—hemlock, cedar, spruce or yellow birch,—one kind alone, or all together, with the bark on; two or three large ones first . . . , and notched at the ends, to the height of three

or four feet, then of smaller logs resting upon traverse ones at the ends, each of the last successively shorter than the other, to form the roof. The chimney was an oblong square hole in the middle, three or four feet in diameter, with a fence of logs as high as the ridge. The interstices were filled with moss, and the roof was shingled with long and handsome splints of cedar, or spruce, or pine, rifted with a sledge and cleaver.[16]

*19th century logging camp in New Brunswick, built in the manner described by Thoreau.*
*Photo from **Emily Weaver's A Canadian History for Boys and Girls,** p. 248.*

Thoreau found the lumber camps to be more primitive than the log houses he came across. There were a few who lived year round in the North Woods, growing potatoes and such for the loggers, or caring for the animals during the off-season. But even with these, Thoreau found the log houses appropriate to the surroundings as if they belonged there and sprouted from the earth itself. Thoreau was clearly struck by the skill of the axeman McCauslin. Thoreau described McCauslin's house as follows:

This house, which was a fair specimen of those on the river [Penobscot], was built of huge logs, which peeped out everywhere, and were chinked with clay and moss. . . . There were no sawed

> boards . . . ; and scarcely any tool but the axe had been used in its construction. The partitions were made of long clapboard-like splints, of spruce or cedar. . . . The roof and sides were covered with the same, . . . and some of a much thicker and larger size were used for the floor. These were so straight and smooth, . . . a careless observer would not have suspected they were not sawed and planed.[17]

The log cabin is indigenous to the North American woodlands. Daniel Beard said of the log cabin, "There is no building which fits so naturally in a wild landscape as a good, old-fashioned log cabin."[18]

If a person could swing an axe and fell trees, a farm was for the claiming. This trend continues to the present: stump farms, wilderness homes, trapper's cabins, logging camps, all built with materials at hand, felled and notched with an axe. For many of us this dream of moving into the great wilderness is still alive, vague whisperings from a heritage that has not been silenced. But vast wilderness is no more and the pockets of wilderness are managed, supervised and regulated. Purchasing land and building a homestead on what had been another's frontier farm in a different century remains a viable option. If one wants a wilderness cabin, perhaps in some ways today it is more complicated, but meanwhile the axe sits in the corner, our link to a simple, honest life.

# FELLING, LIMBING AND BUCKING

*There was a chestnut tree standing close to my log house and leaning toward the building. Under ordinary circumstances felling this tree would cause it to strike the house with all the weight of its trunk and branches. When I told Siley Rosencranz I wanted that tree cut down he sighted up the tree, took a chew of his tobacco, and walked away. For several days he went through the same performance, until at last one day he brought out his trusty axe and made chips fly. Soon the tree was lying prone on the ground pointing away from the house. What this old backwoodsman did was to wait until a strong wind had sprung up, blowing in the direction that he wanted the tree to fall, and his skillful chopping, with the aid of the wind placed the tree exactly where he wished it.*

—D. C. Beard, *Shelters, Shacks and Shanties*

Felling is by far the most dangerous task performed with an axe. It is not the axe, but the tree, that makes it dangerous, and the danger is great no matter if one uses an axe, crosscut or a chain saw. Even an eight-inch diameter tree falls with deadly force. In Maine it is not uncommon to hear reports that a person has died due to a tree having fallen on him or her. Another hazard is the *Widow Maker.* This is a heavy dead limb up high in a tree. As the tree is felled, this limb can snap off, frequently unheard by the feller, and comes crashing down upon his/her head, again with deadly force. Sometimes when a tree starts to fall it gets caught in another tree. People have been killed or injured trying to get a leaner down. Once when I was trying to free a leaner, the tree suddenly kicked free, the trunk sliding over my legs, painfully pinning me down. At first I thought my leg was broken, but I soon realized it was merely twisted in a very uncomfortable position with a very heavy weight resting upon it. I could not budge the tree. I called and called until Claudette heard me hollering. With a peavey we were able to budge the tree enough to free my legs. I was surprised and delighted to find myself able to walk away. I was bruised but beyond that uninjured.

I wish not to discourage anyone who wants to fell trees, but rather to encourage caution. If you have never felled a tree before, do not start with a tree twelve inches in diameter. Start small. A tree roughly six inches in diameter may be just the right size to learn how to fell. In time you will be able to fell that old bull pine, but not now. Acquire the skills first. Don't work where the footing is treacherous or icy. Clear the brush away that may catch the axe as you swing. The deflection caused by the brush could misdirect the bit into your shins or feet.

Don't cut on a windy day; there is no way to predict where the tree will fall. Do not be a beaver cutter, haphazardly chopping around the trunk. This form of cutting, like a windy day, makes it impossible to predict felling direction. Learn to chop the two opposing wedges described

**Room to Swing**

**Don't Stand Behind**

*Two illustrations by Daniel Beard (1914), showing precautions one should take when working with an axe.*

below, always leaving a safety hinge of wood. Make certain you have an escape route and move away as soon as the tree begins to fall. This escape route should be to the side and back. When a tree falls, the springing action of the crown can cause the safety hinge to snap and the butt of the tree to leap from the stump. I witnessed a large bull spruce springing off the stump a good twelve feet high. Anyone standing by that stump could have been killed.

To fell with an axe, one needs to determine the lean of the tree. Do not attempt to make a tree fall in another direction than its natural lean. A tree is too heavy and dangerous to stop once it begins to tip the wrong way. Look at the crown of the tree and the crown of neighboring trees. Can this tree, following its natural lean, move its crown between the others as it falls, or will it become hopelessly hung up? Even if a tree appears to have no lean, look up at the limbs to see if there is a preponderance of weight created by hefty branches growing out mostly on one side of the trunk. Also, look up for large, dead or broken limbs.

With the tree inspected and the direction picked, the felling can begin. The axe should be sharp. If not, touch it up before beginning. The first step is to cut out a wedge one third to half way through the tree. The wedge needs to be on the side of the tree in the direction in which you wish the tree to fall. The wedge cut will literally guide the tree down as it falls. Axes do not cut when striking square to a surface. Always chop at an angle and the chips will fly. Whether felling, bucking, or splitting, the method is a three-stroke procedure. *The first strike is to the far edge, the second is to the near edge, the third is to the center.* The three lower cuts are made followed by three upper cuts. The wedge should be chopped twice as wide as it will be deep. When making the upper cuts, the wedge shape of the axe, itself, causes large chunks to split off. The process is then repeated, chopping deeper into the trunk, until the desired depth is reached.

*The first wedge*

To swing the axe, the right hand is held near the axe head, the left hand holds the foot of the handle at a height even with one's chest. As the axe is swung, the right hand slides down the handle, meeting the left hand just as the axe impacts the tree.

With the wedge cut completed, another wedge must be chopped out on the opposite side. It is extremely important that this wedge be cut a couple inches higher than the first. As the second wedge approaches the first, the tree should start to lean toward the first wedge and when it does, move back and away. Never chop all the way through the tree. Wood is left between the two

*Cutting the second wedge.* ***Note:*** *This is slightly higher than the first.*

wedges, acting as a safety hinge, directing the tree down while holding the falling trunk to the stump.

*A word of warning: When felling a tree that is a heavy leaner, extreme caution should be used in felling.* Never stand directly behind such a leaner while cutting. As the axe severs some of the fibers, the weight can snap the trunk and send the tree catapulting back so fast there would be no time to react. It happened to me. Fortunately, I was out of the way. All I heard was a loud crack and, like a bullet, the tree was down.

With the tree down, work up the trunk limbing. When limbing, strike the underside of the limb where it joins the trunk. Keep the trunk of the tree between you and the limb. This means that as you progress up the trunk, it is necessary to cross back and forth over the trunk. Periodically stop the limbing and clear away the brush. Tripping with an axe is dangerous; so is having brush catch the axe as you swing. Minimizing hazards is the essence of good axemanship. Once the limbing is completed, chop off the safety hinge, freeing the log from the stump.

Sometimes a tree does not fall but becomes hung up in another. There are several ways to get the tree down. The method I least recommend, because of the danger, is to cut the tree it is hung in. Both trees become unpredictable and there is no safe exit. If you have a come-along and some rope, frequently the tree can be winched down. Sometimes chopping the tree free at the stump allows the crown to roll free and fall. Or if it will not roll, a cant hook or peavey may provide enough leverage to roll it free. If all of the above fail, begin the felling process all over again by cutting wedges a few feet above the original wedge. Keep your feet clear, should the tree suddenly buckle where you are cutting. Also, be cautious when the tree falls using this method. The tree may be sprung, and releasing the tension may cause it to spring toward you. This is how my legs ended up pinned beneath a pine. If the tree does not fall after chopping off a few feet higher, repeat the process. Eventually the tree will come down, even if it is piece by piece until no trunk remains. Try not to simply abandon the leaner. It remains a potential hazard that could come down unexpectedly on a windy day.

Bucking a log with an axe is actually less complicated than bucking with a saw (either crosscut or chain saw), because one does not have to worry about the kerf closing on the blade. Even though it is less complicated, it is still physically hard work and whether you find it pleasurable or not will be determined by a few variables. How much wood do you have to buck? How urgently is it needed? How much time can you spare to work at it? And what is your attitude toward physical labor? If you are one whose sedentary job leaves you craving a physical release outdoors in the cool or cold months of the year, this work may be for you. Axe work of this sort is undoubtedly one of the finest forms of exercise there is. A rhythm develops with the arms, back and chest. The lungs fill deeply. There is a feeling of exhilaration, especially out in the frosty air.

Bucking wood is also one of the best ways to learn to use an axe. It is very honest. If not lifted properly, one quickly becomes fatigued. If the cutting angle is too steep, the axe doesn't cut well. If too shallow, the axe glances off and one looks more like a golfer with a follow through swing. When bucking, I prefer an axe with a 36" handle. The longer reach of the handle minimizes back fatigue.

If the logs are for a cabin or fence or something that requires a certain length, the question of where to begin chopping is already answered. If it is simply being bucked into easy lengths for handling, where you start chopping will be where it makes it most convenient for you.

To buck a log, stand on the log with the feet apart. Lift the axe high over your right shoulder. Swing down, letting the axe develop its own momentum. As you swing, the back must also bend, bringing the bit way down onto the forward surface of the log. Strike at somewhere between a thirty-five and forty degree angle. *Remember, the first strike*

*How to buck a log, using an axe*

*is to the upper surface, the second is down as low as you can reach, and the third is struck somewhere between the two.* Swap hand placements, moving the left hand forward while the right hand grabs the foot of the handle. Lift high over the left shoulder. Strike the three blows with an opposing angle, a distance away from the first blows equal to the diameter of the log. These determine the outside edges of the wedge being chopped out. As the axe bites deeper, the right and left hand blows gradually approach one another. Become fluid in the hand swaps, keep true to the chopping angle and the chips will fly. Chop halfway through and stop. Turn around on the log and repeat the process for the opposite side. When the second wedge cut reaches the first, the piece will be severed free. Move up the log and repeat the process at the next point. Competition choppers do not do the hand swap, but cut both to the right and the left with the same hand placement. The style you adopt will be up to you.

During my early years of living in Maine, I owned no chain saw. Though I did fell trees and buck logs to length with an axe when building the 12' by 20' storage cabin, I soon changed the manner in which I worked my woods. I believed that to cut firewood solely with an axe would be rather impractical and wasteful. A good portion of the firewood would be the chips left in the woodlot. In addition to the double bit axe, I began to use a 42" bow saw.

With these two tools I could fell and limb trees, cut the timbers to length, or saw logs into firewood. These met my needs for years, keeping me fit and healthy. If a person owned a small woodlot, used three cords or less per winter, and had sufficient leisure time, a bow saw and axe may be just the ticket. Forty-two-inch bow saws are seldom available today, but thirty-six inch saws can generally be purchased at most hardware stores.

Each of these tools, the bow saw and axe, had characteristics about them that made specific tasks simpler. I would cut out the wedge with the axe, but on the opposite side, rather than chopping out another wedge, I would cut a thin kerf with the bow saw a couple of inches higher than the axe cut. The tree would fall long before binding the kerf ever became an issue.

*Cut wedge with an axe, then do backcut with a bowsaw.*

With the tree down, I would again pick up the axe and limb the tree. Once limbed, the saw was used to cut the log to length. Much of the timber for the house was collected in this way, and for several years all of my fuel needs were met this way too. As the house grew larger, fuelwood needs increased. A wood-heated greenhouse was built. Work and family responsibilities increased to the point that I no longer could find sufficient time to meet my fuel needs working solely with hand tools. Eight cords per year were needed. That is a stack of wood 4' high by 4' wide by 64' long. What had been a joy became an ever-pressing chore. It was at this point that I purchased a chain saw and, like the indigenous woodsman that encounters modern technology, once the chain saw was in my hands there was no going back.

There are times, however, when felling and limbing with only the axe makes sense. Portions of my woodlot are choked with Balsam fir. The fir produces such a heavy, dark, moist canopy that other trees, such as Red Maple and Ash, starved for light, succumb and die. The fir, itself, tends to be a short-lived tree, developing heart rot. I made a decision that if I wanted the hardwoods to prosper, much of the fir would have to be thinned out. Claudette discovered the art of making Christmas wreaths. She soon had a small mail order wreath business going. To supply her with Balsam brush, I would trudge through the snow into the firs with only a double bit axe and some baling twine. I would fell the firs, limb them, collect the brush into bundles, bind them with twine, and carry the bundles back to the house. I would return to the fir trunks in the spring, cutting them into fence posts or firewood, depending upon the need.

Another place in which the axe alone may prove sufficient is if you live in an area with alder, willow or sumac thickets, or you have an overgrown pine thicket with several small dead trees, or you do a lot of camping in places wild enough to have standing and leaning deadwood. You may decide to use breakwood to meet your kindling and campfire needs. Every March I retreat to the woodlot on my days off to make Maple syrup. To fuel the fire and evaporate off gallons and gallons of sap to make syrup, I use breakwood. Breakwood is small dead wood that is broken to length rather than sawn, and there is no better tool for this than the axe. Breakwood is collected tree length and brought to a chopping block. Choke up on the handle of the axe. If using a Hudson Bay pattern axe, choking up on the handle is not necessary. In fact, the Hudson Bay pattern axe is perfect for this work. Lay the piece to be snapped across the chopping block. While one hand holds the stick, the other swings the axe, *striking just beyond the edge of the chopping block.* To strike directly onto the chopping block,

*Making breakwood for sap stove.* ***Note:*** *axe strikes beyond chopping block, giving wood a place to fall rather than spring back.*

there is the danger of the piece springing back into one's face. Striking beyond the block permits the piece to fall to the ground. Generally, the piece breaks free after one or two blows. If not, rotate the stick 180 degrees and strike again. It will snap.

Cutting wood by hand gives one a frugality about wood that drives most chain saw operators insane. Limbwood is not a problem for axes and swede saws, enabling one to use everything down to one or two inches. Leaving far less waste in the woods means having to cut fewer trees to get the same quantity of wood. In this way, a limited woodlot is far less stressed. Limbwood, alders and willows can be ricked up tepee style and left to dry.

Simply take three, tie a tripod and lean the others into the tripod, going round and round. Stacked in this way they will not rot and they need no shelter. The rains and snows just run off. When needed, the alders are dry. Simply chop to length and toss into the stove.

Though I incorporated a saw, whether chain saw or Swede saw, into my firewood cutting, prior to 1850 this would have been foreign practice. Before industrialization, the machine steel necessary to make saws was scarce, expensive and could not be locally forged. On the other hand, virtually every village had a blacksmith. In New England, water-powered trip hammers forged out axe heads. The woodsmen fashioned their own handles. And when the axe bit was worn out, the blacksmith could reopen the iron axe and place in a new steel bit.

Today we saw down trees, saw the wood to length, and only at the last step of the fuelwood scene is the axe used. The sawn billet is stood on end and split with the axe. To a Yankee farmer of 1830, this practice would have been totally backwards and incomprehensible. Collecting fuelwood, the axe was the most important tool if not the only tool. The tree was felled with an axe, chopped to four-foot lengths, and split to size using the axe, a wooden maul and wooden wedges. If a saw was used at all, it was used only to cut these long split pieces to shorter length, before tossing into the woodpile.[19]

# SPLITTING WOOD

*In the Maine woods the woodsmen are adept in making shakes, splits, clapboards, or shingles by the use of only an axe and splitting them out of billets of wood from four to six feet long. . . . an art which only experience teaches. I have seen two-story houses composed of nothing but a framework with sides and roof shingled over with these splits. In the West they call these "shake" cabins.*

—D. C. Beard, *Shelters, Shacks and Shanties*

Wood is split for many reasons, but the most common reason is for fuelwood. Nearly everyone with a stove or fireplace has to do some splitting, and it may be the only reason one even owns an axe.

There is a debate, ongoing, as to whether the best tool for splitting firewood is the axe or the splitting maul. Most would argue that the eight-pound splitting maul is the ideal tool. It has a definite weight advantage and enough girth so that as soon as it penetrates the billet, the block of wood must pop apart. Others would argue equally well that the common felling axe is the ideal tool for splitting wood. Its lighter weight is less taxing on the body. Its sharper, narrower bit penetrates the wood quickly. And it has enough girth to drive the wood fibers apart. I have used both and my preference has drifted from one to the other over time. Currently I am using an 8-pound maul and I love it. A few years ago, however, I would have said I am using a felling axe and I love it.

In the 1970s, during what was called the "Back to the Land Movement," a lot of people returned to burning wood in a big way. The sales of chain saws and wood stoves escalated, and a good deal of literature was written about cutting and splitting firewood. One such book, *The*

*Wood Burners Handbook,* by David Havens in '73, came out strongly in favor of the axe. Havens said, "As for the tools necessary to do the job, the axe seems the most efficient. Some prefer the splitting maul or a sledgehammer and a steel wedge with which to force the wood apart. The axe, once one gets the hang of it, accomplishes the same task with one sharp blow."[20]

David Tresemer of Hand and Foot, Ltd., however, came to a totally different conclusion. He took twenty different tools, including a hydraulic splitter, and tested them on a woodpile. One of these tools was Snow and Nealley's 8-lb. splitting maul. Though the hydraulic splitter slightly beat the maul for time, the Snow and Nealley maul beat out every other splitting tool. Tresemer also compared the pleasantness of the experience. Here he said the Snow and Nealley splitting maul came out way ahead. He described the others as unwieldy, finicky, and the hydraulic splitter as noisy and boring.[21] In Tresemer's analysis, the common felling axe never even made it to the top four finalists. Bruce Cutter of the University of Missouri agrees with Tresemer. Though specifying no particular brand, he states, "For limited production (less than 10 cords per year), studies have shown the best results are achieved with a standard 8-pound splitting maul."[22]

Why did I switch from a felling axe to a splitting maul? The reason is best summed up by the words of Ole Wik, an Alaskan backwoodsman: "Personally, I find it irritating when an axe gets stuck in the end of the chunk of wood that it is supposed to split, as it often does, and I have invested in a splitting maul. The eight-pound head packs a real punch, and the blunt taper makes it almost impossible for the tool to get stuck in the wood."[23]

There are some woods where grain runs straight and true. These woods are easily split. Ash, Oak, and Red Maple frequently have this type of grain. When working with these woods it, perhaps, is easier to split them with an axe. The axe is lighter, there is less fatigue, and the axe slices cleanly into wood of this sort, like a knife into butter. When the grain is twisted, interwoven, forked, has knots, or spongy heartwood, the story can be altogether different. Though the axe is light, compared to the maul, the axe will almost always penetrate the chunk of wood even when it does not have enough force to split the chunk apart. Working with this sort of wood one is repeatedly fighting to lever the axe back out of the block of firewood. Sometimes the axe gets so deeply embedded, especially if the heartwood is spongy, that prying alone will not loosen it. A stick of firewood must be used to knock the axe out of the wood. Whatever pleasure and speed is gained with the axe working in "ideal" wood is lost working with less-than-ideal wood.

The splitting maul is much heavier to use, therefore it takes a greater toll on one's arms and back, but it is too bulky to get wedged in the wood. The splitting maul tends to leave a slight crack and bounce back. The next hit further opens the crack, frequently splitting the block in two. I spend very little time trying to free the maul from a block of wood. I am, however, swinging eight pounds, where, quite often, three pounds would easily suffice.

To split firewood I place the piece to be split upon a low, broad chopping block or stump. The block need not be level because frequently the wood to be split has a slight bevel going this way or that and offsetting the two bevels may assist in having the bolt stand straighter. If it is winter and the ground is snow covered and frozen, I frequently use no chopping block at all. The frozen ground provides adequate support and the compressed snow tends to protect the maul's cutting edge. I would not do this on rocky ground, which surely would damage the maul, but I have found no damage to the bit when it hits icy ground, which is no more dense than the frozen wood. Many, however, would say a block or stump should always be used.

Place the bit of the axe/maul upon the block where you intend to strike. This assures you are the proper distance to strike the wood. An overshoot of the wood is the surest way to snap a handle. With the left hand holding the foot of the handle reach as far forward as is comfortable with the right hand and grab the handle. Stand upright with the feet apart and firmly set. Lift the axe/maul. I tend to lift the axe directly over my head; the splitting maul I tend to lift over my right shoulder. The lifting is actually a sort of controlled tossing in which the right hand is allowed to slide down the handle toward the left hand as the axe/maul goes up. I swing downward, allowing the axe/maul to develop its own momentum. On tough pieces of wood, frequently when working with the axe, I apply additional force to the axe's momentum to create greater impact.

Green wood splits far easier than dry wood. Ideally, wood should be split as soon as it is cut. With small bolts, a single strike to the center should easily pop it in two. On larger pieces it is better to use a one-two-three approach. The first blow should go either to the near edge or the far edge, never the middle. I have noticed that with the splitting maul I always strike the edge farthest away from me first. With the axe, however, I always strike the edge nearest me. The only reason I can give for the difference is that the axe is more apt to become embedded in the

*Starting Position for splitting wood: feet apart, firmly set, right hand near maul.*

wood if my stroke is a little short of the outer edge. The splitting maul seldom gets stuck in the wood. The second stroke, whether axe or maul, is to the opposite edge. (If the near edge was struck first, the far edge should be struck second.) Sometimes the piece pops apart on the second stroke; sometimes it needs a third or fourth stroke. Generally, a crack has begun to form after the second stroke. The third stroke is to the center of the bolt along the forming crack. If it does not split, move again to the far edge and repeat the process. Going to the center on the first blow frequently means repeated blows in which the maul just bounces off or worse. If using an axe, it means wrestling the axe out of the bolt. If the center is slightly punky, either maul or axe can get stuck, and wrestling the tool out of spongy wood can be a real chore, while the blow accomplishes nothing.

Some pieces of wood require a different strategy. A forked trunk is far more difficult to split. To split, place the forked end up. On each fork look for the center pith. To the inside of the pith the grain runs into the

*Maul is tossed up over shoulder as right hand slides down handle.*

*Strike either the near or far edge first.*

fork where it merges with the grain from the other fork. "What God has joined together let no man put asunder." Swing though you might, the fork will not split. Yet, to the outside of the center pith of each branch of the fork, the grain runs clear. Understanding this, a slab can be split from each side by striking to the outside of the piths. Once slabbed, end for end the piece so the fork faces down. Rotate the piece ninety degrees so you are parallel to the fork. In this direction there is no forking of the grain. With the slabs removed, the piece should split with one firm blow to the center.

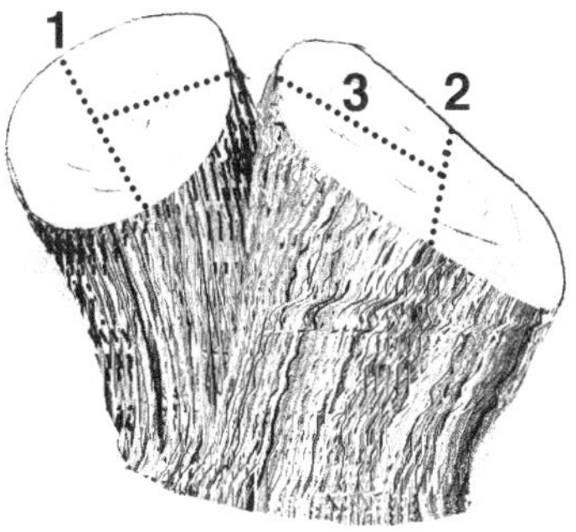


*How to split forked wood. Before doing strike number 3, end-for-end the wood.*

If the bolt has knots, turn them to the left or right of where you intend to strike. You do not want them in line with where you are attempting to split. The grain around a knot twist and the knot itself has grain running in an entirely different direction, making splitting difficult if not impossible. If you think about the meaning of the word knot, you have a clearer picture of what happens to woodgrain around and through one.

Occasionally one comes across a tree, which, in the process of growing, interwove its grain throughout. Such a tree is very difficult to split. Perhaps you have heard people complaining about splitting elm. Elm often grows in the manner just described. The method of trying to open the wood along its radial grain simply does not work. In fact, an axe swung down into the center may, to one's surprise, simply bounce off, creating nothing more than a slight dent. The easiest way to deal with wood of this nature is to slab it.

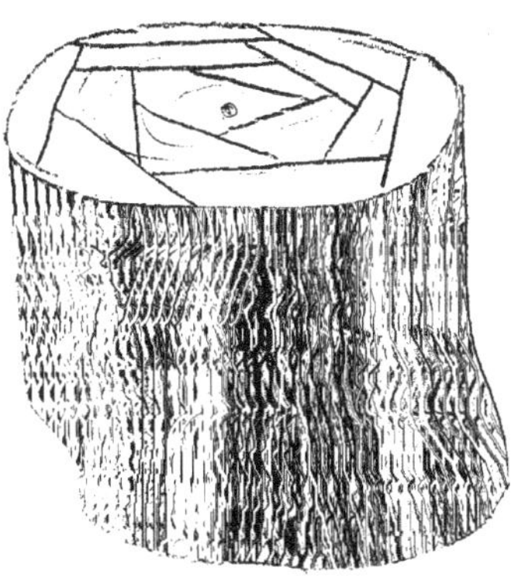

*To split wood with interwoven grain, use the axe or maul to slab the wood rather than trying to split along the radial grain.*

Splitting kindling has its own quirks. If the piece being split can stand on its own, split as for any other piece of wood. If, however, the piece simply will not stand and you must hold the piece as you split it, a greater degree of caution is called for. To split kindling, use a hatchet or choke up on the handle to the point that the axe can easily be swung and controlled with one hand. One hand holds the kindling upright, the other holds the axe so that the bit rests squarely on the wood. Lift both in unison a foot or so above the chopping block and bring them down together, releasing and withdrawing the hand holding the wood as soon as the stick touches the block. The axe continues on through with no risk to the hand.

As soon as we move beyond firewood, many splitting tasks become more than what can be accomplished with the axe alone, but as our predecessors have shown, the axe coupled with accessories the axe can shape are all that is needed. To split a log requires the use of wedges, which can be wooden, and a maul or mallet, which also can be wooden.

*Log-splitting tools: axe, maul, and wedge.*

It takes about five minutes to shape a wedge with a hatchet; about one minute to shape one with a chain saw. Virtually any wood will work. If you have just felled a tree, a section of the crown or limb can yield all the wedges needed. The limb should be around three inches in diameter. The finished wedge should be around ten to twelve inches long. While shaping the wedge, however, it is a good idea to keep it longer and cut it to length when finished. This decreases the risk of striking fingers with the axe. Once the triangular shape has been hewn, saw free and chamfer the sawn edge. Chamfering is simply rounding the sharp corners left by the saw. It is not merely cosmetic. Chamfering extends the life of the wedge by reducing the potential of the wedge splitting from impact. How long a wedge will last is determined by the density of the wood used to make the wedge and the splitability of the logs being worked. When a wedge is no longer functional, toss it into the woodpile and simply shape another. These wooden wedges also work great when felling trees with a chain saw. There is no need to buy expensive plastic wedges when these are so easy to make.

To make a hefty mallet or maul, the densest wood available should be used. The very best mauls are acquired by digging out the root crown of a sapling. The densest wood on my woodlot is Hophornbeam, also called Ironwood. Cut a section from the trunk approximately thirty inches long. If you do not want to dig and chop, cut as close to the ground as possible. The grain spreads and divides as it enters the ground. This wood withstands the continuous pounding better. The butt of this thirty-inch section should be around five inches in diameter.

Determine the length you want for the maul head. Score with knife or axe through the bark so the line is clearly visible. From this line, chop a v-shape all the way around the log, leaving enough wood in the center, slightly greater than the desired diameter of the finished handle.

Stand the maul on the chopping block with the head down. At this point one can work the handle in one of two ways. One can carefully place the axe bit onto the end grain and, with a mallet or hand-held piece of wood, strike the axe into the wood, splitting out the waste wood. One must be cautious not to split deeper the depth of the v-notch or the head of the maul could be split off. Or the waste wood could be chopped off with axe or hatchet. In either case, the final shaping must be done with hatchet and drawknife, crooked knife or pocketknife, until the smoothness and thickness feel comfortable in one's hands. Chamfer any sharp corners on the maul head and it is finished.

*Cutting out notch to protect head while shaping handle.*

*Start split with axe and maul.*

With wedges, a maul, and a single-bit axe, the process of splitting a log can begin. Line the bit of the axe vertically on the center of the butt. Drive the axe into the log by striking the poll with the maul. A crack should begin to run down the log. Insert the wedge into the crack and drive as deeply as it will go. The crack should widen and spread further down the log. The axe generally tumbles out as the split widens. Proceed further down the log, driving in another wedge. Simply continue leap-frogging with the two wedges. As one wedge is driven in, the previous wedge loosens. The loose one can then be pulled and driven further down the log. Continue until the log pops in two. Frequently the axe must be struck into the widening crack to sever stubborn wood fibers holding the two halves together.

*Continue split with wedge.*

Crude planking (*puncheons*) can also be split out, but one must be careful the grain doesn't run off.

*Drive in second wedge, continue leapfrogging with two wedges.*

Keeping the split running true requires not only the wedges but coaxing from the axe's sharp metal bit.

If one has access to a froe, one may want to experiment with splitting shakes. My experience is with making pine shakes. The only tools needed are the froe, froe club and a hatchet. The froe club is essentially identical to the wooden maul previously described only the handle is considerably shorter, designed to be swung with one hand. Like the maul, it should be made of dense hardwood or it will not hold up under use. I am on my second froe club in twenty years of use, and the second club appears to have another 10 years of life left to it.

*Tools required for splitting pine shakes: froe, froe club, hatchet.*

Shakes can be split from pines with diameters as slight as six inches, though ideally the diameter should be from 8" to 14". Greater than 14," the log should be quartered with a sledge and wedge before attempting to split out shingles.

After felling a pine, cut out sections 18" to 20" long between the whorls of knots. Only clear, knot-free wood can be split into shingles. Simply stand the wood on a stump or chopping block. Align the froe across the center of the log. Drive the froe blade in with the froe club as deeply as possible.

Holding the log steady, pull on the froe handle until the log snaps

Driving froe into knot-free, 18" long pine bolt.

into two halves. Take each half and halve again. Continue halving until the thickness is about 1". To assist the splitting, I frequently push the bottom of the bolt with my knee as I pull the froe handle towards me.

When the bolt is slightly over one-inch thick, I make the final split. The froe is carefully centered and driven in. I hold the top of the bolt tightly together with one hand while I press with my knee against the bolt, controlling the split by pushing or pulling the froe handle as I work downward. The split tends to run in the direction force is applied. If the split is worked properly, and the force is applied correctly, you should be rewarded with two shingles. If

*Final split: carefully center froe. Tap froe into shake (below). Hold top tightly together, press knee against shakes and control split by pushing and pulling on handle of froe while working froe down (right).*

not, the grain will run out ruining one of the two shingles. With practice this gets easier.

Some trimming of rough edge grain irregularities can be taken off with froe and club by placing the froe upon the material to be removed and striking.

*Trim off bark and high points.*

*A finished shake.*

*Pine shakes on a log house.*

*Roof being covered with pine shakes.*

Trim off the bark and any noticeable high points with hatchet and stack to dry. They dry quickly. I nail them up with galvanized 5d box nails. For walls, I leave eight inches exposed. For roofs, I leave six inches exposed. For shaking a roof, I consider a 9:12 pitch perfect. It is not too steep to work on but it is steep enough to insure quick shedding of water. On roofs I prefer to nail the shingles to 1" by 3" furring strips to allow for air flow beneath the shingles, promoting quicker drying and adding to the overall life of the shakes.

# AXE MAINTENANCE

*My axe had come off and I had cut a green hickory for a wedge, driving it in with a stone.*

—Thoreau, *Walden*

Before one considers using an axe, an inspection of its condition is necessary for one's own protection. Is the blade sharp? Is the head seated tightly? Is the handle sound?

If the blade is dull, a condition very likely to exist on an axe used primarily for splitting firewood, it becomes a liability, especially when being used for pointing, limbing, hewing or felling. A dull axe, when it should bite, is more likely to glance off its target, putting the user's shins and feet at risk. When routinely sharpened, the job takes but a few minutes and only a flat file is required.

From time to time I sharpen my axes using an electric grinding wheel. This is considered a crime by some people. I cannot recommend the use of an electric wheel unless one is very proficient at axe sharpening and knows the proper face angle that must be preserved. The axe is a tool that requires great impact in order to be effective. That is the reason for the long handle and the poll. In order for the cutting bit to withstand this impact, the shape of the cutting bit must be kept convex. Working with an electric wheel, which can remove a considerable amount of metal quickly, there is a risk that the cutting edge will be hollow ground or concave. Such a cutting edge will not hold up in use.

Another risk in using an electric wheel is the danger of over-heating the metal and ruining the temper. When using an electric wheel, the bit should be *frequently dipped into water* to keep it from getting too hot.

A fine cutting edge can be put on with a stone, but the easiest way to sharpen an axe is to use a 10" or 12" mill bastard file. The surface of the file should appear dull. If the surface of the file is shiny, the cutting ability of the file may no longer be effective and a new file may have to be purchased. These are available at any hardware store and a quality file can be purchased for under ten dollars. It will give years of service. You can also purchase files at old tool stores, but I don't recommend it. A worn file is useless and that, unfortunately, is quite likely to be the case with these bargain files.

To sharpen, place the axe flat upon a table or your knee with the bit protruding. The nice part about using your knee rather than a table is that your knee is always with you, enabling you to sharpen your axe anywhere, including out in the woods. Secure the head by pressing down upon the poll with the back of the left palm while allowing the fingers to cup gently over the file, assisting in guiding the cut of the file. With the file in the right hand, push the file across the bevel, moving from the bit toward the poll and slightly to the right with each pass. The first few passes, metal should be removed not from the cutting edge, but from the bevel along its entire length. In order to keep the original cutting shape of the axe, it is necessary to trim back the bevel slightly every time the axe is sharpened. If the file is sharp, the area the file has worked should shine as new metal is exposed. Once the bevel has been slightly thinned, rotate the file ever so slightly to the cutting edge to thin out a fine edge. Flip the axe and repeat the process on the other side. Lightly file off any filing burrs from the new edge and the axe should be ready to use. A final honing can be done with a fine oilstone or leather strop if you are so inclined.

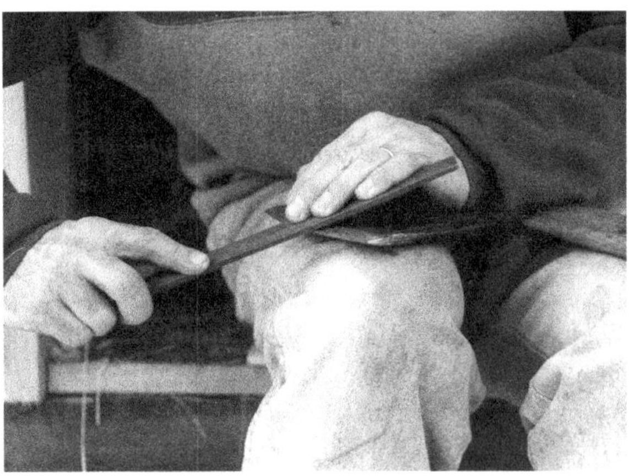

*Sharpening an axe with a 10" flat mill file.*

If the bit has peened over nicks from having hit a rock or metal, these should be filed flat before the general filing is done. A nick, however, left in the blade will not greatly affect the axe's performance provided any peening has been properly removed. Check the edge with

*A table top can also be used to steady the axe while sharpening with a file.*

the finger tips. Do not slide the fingers, but rather touch. A very sharp axe is apt to cut the fingers much the same way a knife would if the fingers were slid across the edge. Another way to check the quality of one's sharpening is to hold the cutting edge to the light and look for reflected light. A properly sharpened edge has no flat surfaces, therefore it reflects no light.

When dealing with a loose head, we are potentially dealing with a life-threatening hazard, especially if someone else is in the general area where the axe is being used. An axe is swung with great force. Should the axe fly off in such a swing, it would be catapulted with deadly velocity. An emergency solution with a camp axe, for example, where no wedges may be available, is to soak the axe in water, swelling the wood fibers of the handle until the axe holds firm. Such a solution, however, is strictly for emergency, for once the wood dries out, it will be looser than before the soaking. The best solution by far is to drive in a metal wedge. These are available at any hardware store where axe handles are sold.

One of the easiest ways to create a loose axe is to treat the axe like a wedge or hammer. When the bit is simply driven into a billet and the axe is pounded with a sledge hammer until the firewood pops, or when the poll of the axe is used to drive a metal wedge, the metal to metal impact slowly changes the shape of the axe, compressing the length of the eye while increasing the width. When the width expands beyond a certain threshold, the handle will not grab the sides of the metal, nor will a commercially made replacement handle grab the metal sides because the problem is not with the handle; it is with the axe. There is a solution to even this problem, but the abusive practice of metal-to-metal impact has to cease or the expanding eye will develop a crack in which there is now the danger of the axe shattering upon impact. A person wishing to handle an axe with a widened eye can make a handle, giving it the extra width needed to fit. And if in your wood splitting scene there is still a need to use the axe as either a hammer or wedge, have the contact be metal to wood by using wooden wedges called "gluts" or a large wooden club called a maul. Instructions for making a glut and a maul are covered in the section "Splitting Wood."

In the case of a cracked handle, we again have an emergency situation. Cracks tend to run along grain lines, so with grain lines running along the length of the handle, they are reparable. If the crack is minor, the handle can be repaired with tape. The tape I am talking about is a black, cloth tape that is extremely cohesive (sticks to itself). The brand name I recall is "Bulldog" tape. As a boy playing sandlot baseball, the one possession I feared would get broken was my wooden baseball bat. In sandlot baseball the bat was always a scarce resource. To protect the bat where it was most vulnerable, we would wrap the handle with this tape. To this day I use the tape for any small cracks that form, or to protect the handle where it shows the most wear. With axes and splitting mauls used to split firewood, this wear is generally to the handle directly beneath the axe. If wrapped tightly, with each course of tape overlapping all but one quarter to three eights of an inch, the axe handle can be strengthened almost to its original strength.

If the crack is fairly long, and it looks doubtful tape alone will suffice, attempt the following: drill two small holes through the handle, one near where the crack begins and one near where it ends. If glue can be injected into the crack, do so. Push through each hole a 6d nail and fit a small washer over the pointed end. Snip off the point, leaving a little protruding beyond the washer. With the head of the nail resting on something iron, like a vise or splitting wedge, peen the snipped end flat so that it mushrooms out against the washer, pulling in tight to the handle. With the crack now riveted back together, wrap as described above.

Should the break be unrepairable, it is time to fit a new handle. Frequently, the most difficult task is removing the old handle. Cut off the old handle flush with the axe.

Place a 3/8" or 1/4" twist bit into either an electric or hand drill. If a hand drill is used, it becomes necessary to place the axe into a vise or clamp because both hands are needed to operate the hand drill. Also, do not use a bit designed solely for boring wood; striking the metal sides or hitting a metal wedge would ruin the bit. The standard twist bits are designed for working metal. Starting with the sawn-off end, begin boring as much wood out of the eye as is possible, avoiding the metal wedges where feasible. Repeat the process through the top.

The boring should not simply be a straight, perpendicular hole. One should bore at various angles so that one hole tunnels across another, severing the continuity of the handle completely so that, when tapped, it tumbles out in pieces. Sometimes, when sufficiently bored, the remains of the handle simply fall out. Other times, the remains must be tapped out from the underside with either a metal rod or blunted spike. If after being tapped, the handle still persists, more boring is required. Check that no wood remains in the eye, and salvage the metal wedges from the refuse; these can be refitted into the new handle.

Some people do not drill out the old handle, but, instead, char the handle until it comes out. This method is fail safe as far as removing the old handle is concerned. The wood will burn out, the metal will remain, but such a practice may have cost the axe itself. I have seen an axe heated until the steel glowed reddish-yellows. The charred, glowing ember of a handle simply fell out, but the axe had lost its temper, making it not much stronger than some of the wood it would be striking. Steel that has been overheated and allowed to cool slowly will not hold an edge and will easily peen and chip on contact with something hard.

If you were foolish enough to destroy the axe's temper, do not destroy the axe by trying to use it in this condition. The axe must be retempered. To retemper, reheat the axe until it again glows reddish-yellow. Remove from the heat and quickly quench it in water. The quick cooling locks carbon in the steel and hardens it. To ensure the axe was not over-hardened, the axe can be put onto a regular oven rack and the oven turned up as high as it will go. This will help keep the axe malleable.

When purchasing a handle, avoid buying seconds. Generally, these are seconds because of defective grain patterns that could crack or shear in use. Check the grain lines closely. What is desired are nice long, smooth-flowing grain lines that show no sign of run-off. The color of the wood should be light. The wood of choice is hickory, generally the wood sold. Pick it up and see how it feels. It is your hands that will be sliding along this wood. Look at it from various angles. It should run straight and true, not bowed or twisted. Handles usually have a wedge attached. If not, find out where they are kept, as one of these will be needed when setting the handle.

Buying a handle for an axe is not the same as buying a nut for a bolt. Whereas the latter simply goes together, the handle frequently does not fit the eye. Often it must be carefully rasped or whittled before it will fit. This requires periodic checking, rasping, rechecking to remove just enough wood from just the right area so the handle has a nice (not loose) fit.

At this point remove the handle, insert the wooden wedge into the handle slit, and reinsert it into the eye. One easy way to set the handle is to hold the head while driving the butt of the handle against a log, stump or floor until it slides through the eye and is flush with the top of the axe.

The reason I suggest starting the wedge prior to fitting is because sometimes, after driving the handle, the slit closes so tightly the wooden wedge cannot be started. With the handle now flush with the axe and the wedge protruding, drive the wedge as deeply as possible. Cut off the remainder and follow this by driving two small metal wedges at an acute angle across the wooden wedge. In this way the already tight wood fibers have been forcefully pushed in all directions, a fit that should last many years. (Many axe handles today come with a single large aluminum wedge rather than a wooden wedge and two small metal wedges.)

*Fitting handle by hitting butt against stump.*

Perhaps instead of purchasing a handle, it strikes your fancy to make your own. This is not as difficult as it seems, and, in truth. an axe handle can be shaped with no other tools than a hatchet and a pocket knife. The correct names for an axe handle are *helve* and *haft*, words derived from Old English meaning

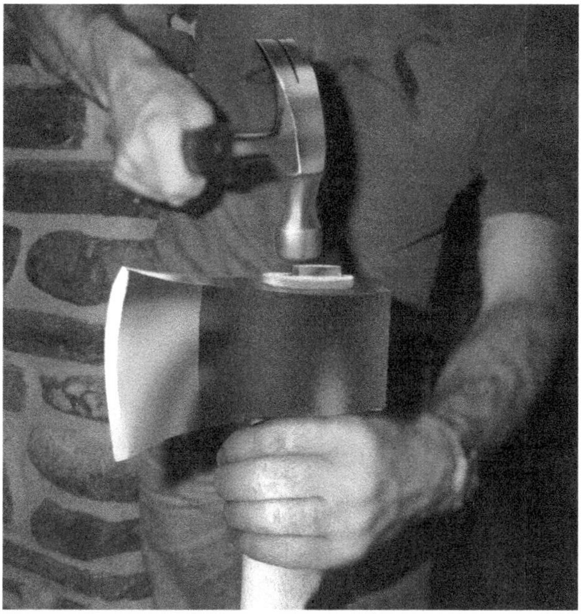
*Driving a wedge*

halve, and these name describes the process involved in making a handle. A length of tree trunk 28" to 36", depending on personal preference, is needed. The type of wood chosen is also personal preference. The favored wood for impact handles is Hickory. If Hickory does not grow in your area, Ash is usually considered. In Scandinavia, Birch is used. Calypso used olive wood. I've seen Maple used. I have used Ash, Red Oak, and Hophornbeam. Hophornbeam is the hardest, densest wood growing here in Maine. I don't know much about its shock value to my arms, but I seldom have to replace one of these handles due to breakage.

The finest helves come from straight-growing trunks seven inches or better in diameter. These trunks are split into eights or more and the darker wedge of heartwood along with the sapwood is split off.

If one wishes to keep the process even simpler, serviceable handles can be made by simply splitting a four- or five-inch-thick sapling in half and making two handles. This type of handle may be inclined to warp. If one wishes a slight curve and a coltsfoot as is found in commercial handles, look for a tree that has this as its natural configuration. Such a tree will make the strongest handle.

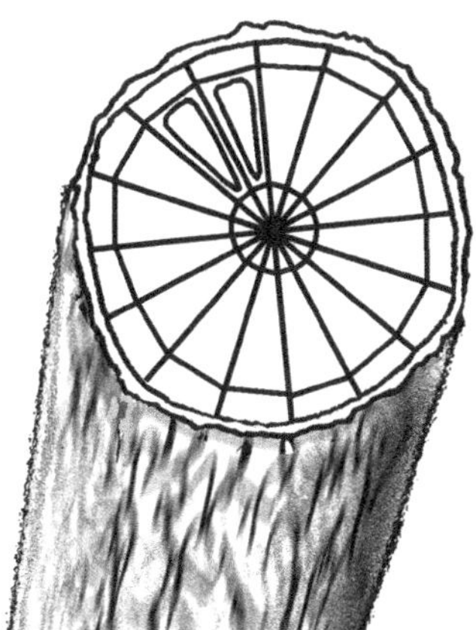
*To make handles: cut wood to proper length, split along radial grain, split off sap - wood and heartwood, shape handle.*

*Axe fitted with Hophornbeam handle.*
*Handle was shaped from naturally curved and bent section of trunk, creating a strong handle with no runoff grain.*

Once cut and brought to the wood-working area, it should be worked as soon as possible, before the wood checks, rendering it good for only firewood. To split the bolt, stand it on end, place the bit of the axe clearly across the center line. (If you have a froe, that would work even better than the axe.) Pound the axe into the bolt with a wooden mallet. If no mallet is available, use a stick of firewood. Once the poll is completely buried into the trunk, tap on the protruding handle, driving it deeper. Be careful not to pound so hard as to damage the handle. At this point, grab the top of the bolt with one hand while still holding the axe handle with the other. Give the axe handle a quick sideward jerk (again be careful not to jerk so hard as to snap the handle). This quick jerk should provide the necessary leverage to pop the bolt in two. If this fails, simply drive a wedge or glut further down into the crack and that should split it.

*Draw the pattern of the handle onto the newly split surface.*

Draw the pattern of the handle you wish to make onto the newly split surface. If you are copying an already existing handle, simply lay this on the wood and trace it. If you have no sample, simply free-hand a pattern onto the wood so that with quick visual reference you know how much wood to remove with axe or hatchet. Draw the section that fits the eye larger than needed. You want to leave considerable wood at the top of the handle to allow for shrinkage that will occur during seasoning.

There is an ongoing debate as to whether S-curved handles are better than straight handles. Prior to the Civil War, most people made their own handles, and most axe handles were straight. After the Civil War, with the advent of a particular type of lathe, the curved handle became more fashionable. Mathematicians and Physicists may be able to demonstrate why the curved handle is an advantage, delivering more impact with each swing, but I still find it hard to accept that the curve matters at all. If I look at the axe that became the standard in logging camps in the late 19th century, I find it is the straight handled, double-bit axe. If the curved handle reduces the labor involved in felling trees, why would the logging industry choose a straight handle? For me, the handle shape comes down to personal preference. I have made both straight and curved handles.

Once the pattern is drawn upon the helve, place the billet upright onto a stump or block and commence hewing with the hatchet. Remove as much wood as possible, being careful not to remove wood beyond the pencil line. Also, as you develop your sculpturing skills, you need to

*Final shaping of axe handle with pocket knife.*

note in which direction the wood hews off cleanly and in which direction it tears and chafes. As we approach the pencil line, avoid striking in the direction that causes the grain to tear or you may tear into your handle. This may sound confusing, but as you work the wood it becomes obvious. By the time you've worked the wood down to the pencil line you should have a pretty clear idea of your skills with the hatchet and on how the grain runs. Carefully, with the hatchet, shape the roundness to the handle. Do it with lighter and shorter strokes.

The finish work is done with a drawknife, a crooked knife, or a pocket knife, and smoothed until the handle has a comfortable feel. The same applies to the knife as applies to the hatchet: in one direction the wood tends to strip away cleanly; in the other direction, it tears. Attempt, as much as possible, to work the grain in its favorable direction.

The head of the helve, which was drawn oversized, should be roughly hewn oversized and not finished with the knife at this time. Put the unfinished helve away to season for a couple of months. Once seasoned, carefully finish shaping the head. The final fitting can be done with a rasp as was previously described. A cut needs to be sawn into the edge grain, 2 to $2^1/_2$ inches deep. This cut needs to be very straight and centered. It will hold the wooden wedge.

You can make your own wooden wedges if you choose. They can be sawn with a backsaw from a small piece of lumber, or cut from a chunk

*To shape an offset Broadaxe handle,*
*pour boiling water onto green handle, and clamp to the desired shape.*

of firewood (which is how I acquired mine). If you have access to a band saw, the task of cutting out wedges is very simple. The other option is to buy a wooden wedge for every handle made. In either case, one still needs a couple of metal wedges.

If you are trying to make an offset handle for a Broadaxe, while the handle is green, secure the head of the handle to a table with a C clamp. Make certain that the whole portion that is to fit into the axe is flat on the table. Pour boiling water onto the handle. Insert a wood-splitting wedge under the handle, about a foot from the C clamp. Using another clamp, bring the foot of the handle down slightly so that it is parallel with the head, yet a couple of inches off the table. Allow the handle to sit like this for a week or two. When the clamps are released, the handle will have the offset shape. As with the regular handle, the head should be oversized and permitted to fully season before fitting onto the axe.

If by chance you have completely ignored my instructions concerning seasoning the handle before fitting, you have, within weeks, come to the realization that you have a rather serious problem. I speak, embarrassingly, from experience. The shrinkage can be so great that voids may actually appear around what was a tight fit. To save, attempt the following: Fill the voids with epoxy, plunging the epoxy into the voids with a finish nail, toothpick, or something fine. Once the voids will take no more epoxy, permit the epoxy to dry, then drive in one or two additional wedges. This should correct the haste and secure the axe, though such a solution remains no substitute for patience. Understandingly, the desire to make an axe helve is strongest when the only one we had is the broken end protruding from the axe. At such times, seasoning two minutes may be all you are willing to wait. Heed the scout motto: Be prepared. Make an axe handle while the other is still functional.

# HEWING

*So I went on for some days cutting and hewing timber, and also studs and rafters, all with my narrow axe . . .*

*I hewed the main timbers six inches square, most of the studs on two sides only, leaving the rest of the bark on, so that they were just as straight and much stronger than sawed ones.*

—Henry David Thoreau, *Walden.*

Hewing is the process by which the rounded surface of a log is removed, leaving an axe-flattened surface. A tree trunk can be hewn down to a square timber, making it easier to use in construction. Hewing is neither chopping nor splitting wood. Hewing is slicing away wood. In hewing, we work with the grain; but unlike splitting, we do not follow the grain.

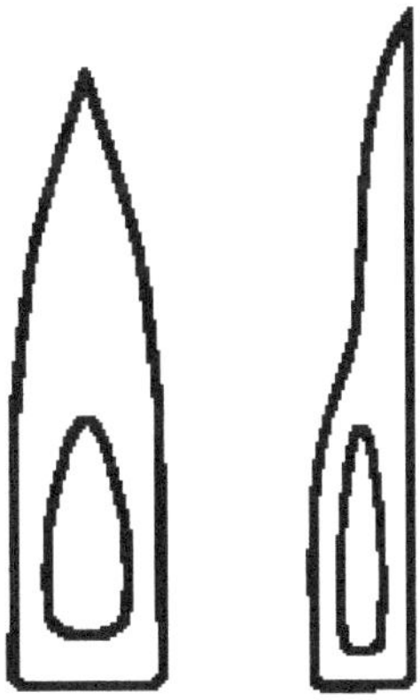

*Double beveled, and chisel-faced single beveled.*

The methods of hewing are incredibly varied. Almost anything I can say about hewing tools, stance, or style can easily be contradicted by another. Some of the variables affecting method are the size of the timber, the height off the ground in which the timber is being hewn, where the timber is hewn, the axe used, the equipment available to move the log, and personal preference for safety. I can say, for example, that the traditional tool for hewing is the chisel-faced Broadaxe, but the hewing axe I originally learned to hew with was double-beveled.

The availability of used double-beveled-pattern hewing axes tells me that many hewers in Maine used double-beveled axes. The simple reality is, as Thoreau stated and countless pioneers prove, no other tool but the common felling axe is necessary to create acceptable hewn timbers.

*A log dog holding a log steady for hewing.*

Very few tools are needed, and all are easy to come by. Needed are a few odd nails and a couple of scrap boards around 3' in length, a hammer, chalkline, tape measure, pocketknife, and a small level. If you own a log staple (log dog) or two, you do not need the boards. A log staple looks like its namesake. It is a heavy metal staple. One point is driven into the log, the other is driven into a crib log. This holds the log steady while it is being scored and hewed.

The other tools needed are a basic felling axe, a Broadaxe (if you have one) and a drawknife. Some hardware stores carry drawknives, some do not. Old tool places tend to have them, and generally every tool catalog sells them. The drawknife is an excellent tool for peeling off the remaining bark after the hewing process. Summer-cut wood, when the sap is up, can usually be peeled without the knife, but winter-cut wood is difficult; the bark clings to the wood. The drawknife is a must when peeling in autumn or winter.

*Drawknife*

One problem with logs is that they are heavy, particularly when green. That is, however, the best time to work the log. Green wood cuts easier than seasoned logs, and it is imperative that the bark is not left on a log lying upon the ground during the summer months or the log is likely to become home for wood-boring insects. I own neither a skidder, tractor, nor truck. Getting green logs out of the woods to be hewn is an impractical, if not near impossible, solution for me. In dealing with the above problem I have come up with some conclusions that seem to run contrary to

*Bark can simply be pulled from summer cut wood without using drawknife.*

what many contemporary hewers have recommended. To me, the most logical place to hew a timber is in the woods where the tree has fallen. This eliminates the need to lift the heavy log altogether. Once hewn and peeled, the timber is already lighter. Prop each end up by setting the timber on short lengths of log and let it air dry. When ready to use in a few weeks it is amazing just how light the timber is compared to the heavy log we started with. Balancing the seasoned timber on a garden cart, two people can easily walk a 30' beam out of the woods. By myself, I have taken out a 6" by 12" twenty-three-feet-long using the cart.

A hewn timber need not be hewn square. The number of surfaces flattened, and the angle of one surface to another is determined by use and aesthetics of the finished structure. Floor joists need only one flattened surface, leaving the remainder round. This may or may not compliment the rest of the structure, but it depends on what one is building. When building a post and beam frame, the timbers generally should be squared. With all the pockets, tenons, mortises, and laps to be cut, and all the fitting and pegging to be done, the flat surfaces facilitate measurement.

*Moving a 28-foot timber from woods to house with garden cart.*

The hewn log house frequently has only two surfaces flattened, bringing the log to a common thickness of 6" or 8", while the top and bottom surfaces are left in the round. This gives the structure plumb walls inside and out.

Another style of log building that would require only 2 surfaces being hewn is to lay the flattened surfaces one onto the other, permitting the round surfaces to become the internal and external walls. Self-expanding weather stripping could be laid between the courses, making

*Squared 6"x10" timber.*

*Small cabin built of hewn logs.*

weather-tight walls. Corners in such a building could be joined using traditional joinery or simply butt joined and spiked, as is often done today with many commercial log homes.

With the necessary tools in hand, the hewing process can begin. Up here in the Northeast we are blessed with an amazing diversity of trees for building. I use predominantly white pine.

Select a tree slightly thicker than the desired dimension. This is sometimes a difficult guess because the tree must be slightly thicker at the narrow end which, for a 28' log, is quite a ways up there. If there is a small log around, place this where you intend to fell the tree. This will help keep the trunk directly off the ground, helping to preserve the bit of the hewing axe. Fell the tree. Free it from the stump and cut the butt flush. Measure off the desired length and make a slash with axe or knife. Limb up to and slightly beyond this slash but no further.

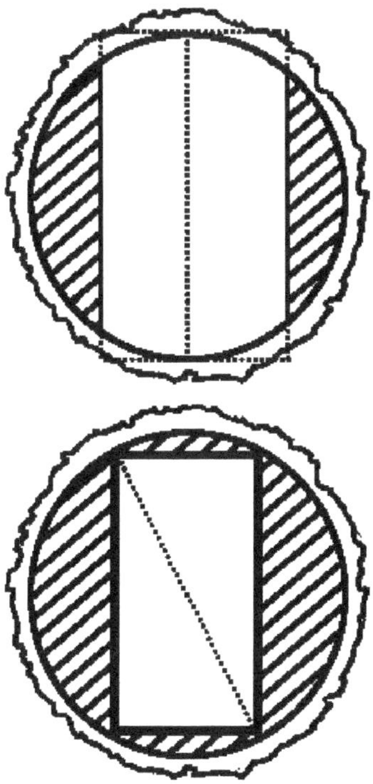

*How thick does the tree have to be? If rounded corners are acceptable, the diameter of the tree at the narrow end need only match the desired width of the finished timber. If a 6"x10" is desired, the narrow end of the log must be 10 inches wide (top).*

*If perfectly square corners are desired, the Pythagorean theorem must be used to calculate the log dimension required: $a^2+b^2=c^2$. In such a case, a 6"x10" would require a log slightly over 12" thick at the narrow end (bottom).*

When I first started hewing I copied what I found other hewers doing in books. I used log cribs with pockets notched out in the cribs to hold the log. As I scored or hewed the log, it had a tendency to turn, sometimes leaving me with a corkscrew timber if I wasn't paying attention. I added scrapwood nailers to hold the log. The nailers worked relatively well, but I still was not satisfied.

One day after felling a tree, but before limbing, I was struck with a realization. With the crown limbs still attached, the log was incapable of rolling. It was not necessary to secure the log. All that was needed was to keep it attached to its own

*Tree felled across a log to keep trunk clear of the ground. Crown remains attached, keeping tree from rolling while being hewn.*

stabilizer, the crown. Of course, this is only good for hewing the first two sides, after which the log must be sawn or chopped from the remainder of the tree to do the last two surfaces. The log, however, after the first two sides are hewn, can now rest upon a flattened surface, which in itself will resist turning and, once secured with nailers, will not move.

Measure the width across the butt. Mark the center. Using a small level, make a vertical line through the center. This line becomes the reference line for the end lines. If you are attempting to get a 6" by 8" beam from a log with a 12" diameter at the butt, six inches of wood will be removed. Draw a vertical line, using the level, 3" to each side of the center line. Double check that these two lines are indeed six inches apart. Make a notch with the knife at the top, through the bark. This will help with establishing where to snap the chalkline.

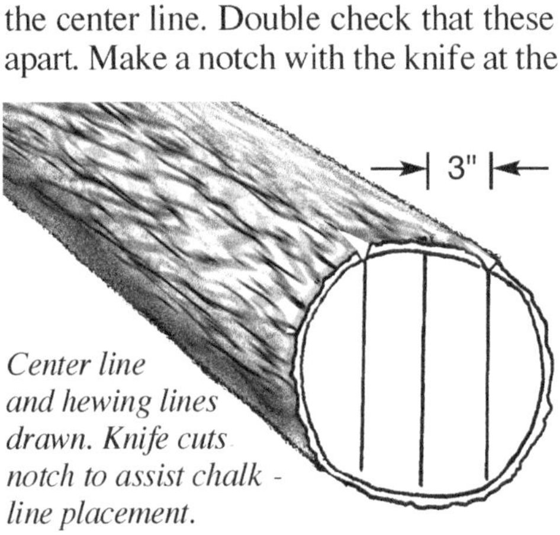


*Center line and hewing lines drawn. Knife cuts notch to assist chalk-line placement.*

Proceed up the trunk to the top of the timber. This will either be clean cut with the saw if nailers and cribs are used, or it will be a slash across the trunk if the crown remains attached to the trunk. Mea-

*On a straight log, the wood to be removed is equal on each side (above). On a bowed log, when snapping a chalkline, it sometimes is necessary to mark all the wood to be removed on a single side of the tree butt (below).*

sure the diameter here. Mark the midpoint into the tree bark using the knife (if crown remains attached; if not, mark in the same manner as the butt). Measure 3" from each side of the knife mark. Mark through bark with knife. Double check that the two opposite marks are 6" from one another. Insert a 5d or 6d nail into the knife notch. Drape the chalkline ring over it. Walk back with the chalkline to the notch on the log butt. Pull the line taut and snap it. The pull should be straight up and down for that is the plane we are to remove. Repeat for the notches on the opposite side of the log. Put away the nail and chalkline and grab the axe.

*Prior to hewing, this log was bowed. Note how close the center pith is to the right edge.*

There are circumstances when the center of the log would not be used as the basis for measurement. Rather, virtually all the wood to be removed would be removed from a single side of the log. A bowed log would be an example of this.

Before hewing, the log must be scored. Scoring is vertically slashing, chopping or sawing the wood to the chalkline. I use two methods to score.

The first method I use involves the use of only an axe. I stand on the log with feet apart and I chop to the chalkline. It is not necessary that the wood be removed in the scoring process; it is only necessary that the axe penetrate to the chalkline.

*Scoring to the line with an axe. A long-handled axe helps.*

Novice hewers tend to not score deeply enough. Properly scored, hewing requires surprisingly little effort. Continue up the log, chopping every few inches. Strike to the top, the bottom and the middle. Large chips should flake off as you score. When you're done, turn around and score down the other line. As you go along, special effort should be given to chopping knots out. If the diameter of the log is small, standing on the log may be either inconvenient or precarious. In which case, simply stand behind the log to score rather than standing on it.

*When properly done, large chips flake off.*

*Scoring to the chalkline with a chain saw while straddling log. Care must be taken not to saw beyond the chalkline or chain saw marks will be left on the hewn timber.*

The second method I use involves both a chain saw and an axe. In this method, the vertical scoring cuts are sawn with a chain saw and the chunks of wood between the saw cuts are chopped out with the axe. Saw kerfs are spaced about every four or five inches.

Once the chunks between the kerfs have been chopped off, the surface may need to be lightly rescored with the axe prior to hewing it cleanly with the Broadaxe.

I went through a long period of time when I did all of my scoring with a felling axe. When I made the transition from scoring with an axe to scoring with a chain saw and axe I completely abandoned my old method of just using the axe, but over the years the axe method has come back to me. The deciding factor on whether or not to use the chain

*Hewing, standing to right of log, left foot back, right foot forward, right hand forward on axe handle. With this stance the hewer's eyes are parallel with hewn edge.*

saw in scoring is how much wood has to be removed. If the thickness can easily be chopped through with a felling axe, I do not use the chain saw. If the scoring process would be long, tedious and difficult, I'd use the chain saw. On a large log, the chain saw is an amazing labor saver.

Up to a few years ago, when I hewed, I straddled the log. I continue to find that many people prefer to straddle the log. In the last few years, however, my stance has changed. I find the easiest stance for hewing is to stand with both feet to the right of the log. Put the left foot back, the right foot forward. The left hand holds farther back on the handle while the right hand holds close to the axe head. With a single beveled Broadaxe, the handle should be an offset handle curved away from the log, or you will be skinning your knuckles.

To hew with any axe, one needs to get a feel for the bevel. This is especially so with a double-beveled axe. The intent is to remove the wood and create a flush surface. That is why the traditional Broadaxe has no bevel on its inner surface, but is flat like a chisel. If a double-beveled axe is used, the axe must be pivoted slightly so that the bit's beveled surface becomes the flush, chiseling surface.

If the angle is too great, the axe chops instead of hews. If it is too shallow, the axe glances off. If correct, the scored chips just peel away, leaving the flush bare wood surface. The point of contact should be, as near as possible, directly even with the lead foot. Should the axe glance from the log, it will continue traveling. That is why the lead foot must be away from the path of the axe.

When working with the Broadaxe, I slice across the wood at a steep angle.

Work the log from front to back, hewing along the chalkline. As the scored pieces pull back, a natural kerf is formed, almost guiding the axe. Any knots encountered will require additional force if they were not sufficiently scored, but if all was done properly the hewing process will be a joy. For light, controlled strokes, slide the lead hand further up the handle toward the axe head. For less controlled, more forceful strokes, slide the hand further down the handle. The forceful strokes clean out the material; the light strokes create the clean hewn surface.

Hew up one side of the tree and down the other. If only two sides need to be hewn, simply cut it free and it is done. If the timber needs to be squared, flip it. Check that the hewn surface (now facing up) is level. Snap chalklines, score and hew as before.

Peel the beam as soon it is finished. Keep it propped off the ground. If it is a long beam, it is a good idea to also prop up the middle. If the remainder of the tree has another useful beam in it, repeat the process all over again. If not, cut the useable tops into cordwood. Stack the wood and pile the brush. There is no reason to be out there in the woods tripping over tops and brush. In a few weeks of work, several golden beams will be quietly seasoning in the woodlot.

*The timeless beauty of the hewer's craft is attested to by this home reconstructed in the Great Smokey Mountains.*

# HEWING AS CRAFT AND TRADE

*Great Mast houses were put up at the mouth of Saco river, and many workmen employed there for years, until the war of the Revolution.*

*Those who were employed in the forest, cutting and hauling the enormous trees, were called "masters" and "mastmen," while those who hewed and dressed them, in the long sheds built for that purpose, were designated "mast-wrights."*

—G. T. Ridlon, Sr., *Saco Valley Settlements and Families,* Portland, Maine, 1895, p. 213

When I think about the axe and the ability to derive income through axemanship, there are actually few possibilities that arise. If I were to compare the difference of appearance from wood split with a maul to wood split with a hydraulic splitter, the difference, if in fact there was any, would not be worth the additional price I would want to charge as a Master splitter. Splitting wood with a maul does not noticeably enhance the appearance of firewood, and even if it did, it would probably be irrelevant. It is also irrelevant whether one fells a tree with an axe or a saw. The axe-chopped tree butt has no more value than one felled with a chain saw.

Axemanship can only survive as a saleable trade where the aesthetics of the finished piece cannot be duplicated in a mechanized fashion. Hand-split shakes and hewn timbers have such aesthetic appeal. Where hewn timbers are placed within a house, they define the character of the space.

Sawn timbers could not be substituted for hewn timbers and create the same effect. The value of hewn timbers over that of sawn timbers is

*With the house finished,*
*hewn timbers become the house's most notable aesthetic feature.*

*The hewn timbers define the space.*

*Even a simple timber frame as this . . .*

*. . . can have dramatic effects such as this.*

obvious when one considers that many hewers and log builders are purchasing sawn dimensional timbers and hewing the surface so that the timbers appear hewn.

Old Virginia Log Homes specializes in hewn-log-home kits. The hewn logs are 6" by 12" white pines. These come to Virginia Log Homes sawn out. Working with common felling axes, the sawn surface is hewn away, creating, as with all double-beveled axe hewing, an attractive rippled surface. Old Virginia Log Homes confirms what Thoreau stated. Only a simple felling axe is necessary if one wants hewn timbers.

In 1982 Drew Langsner published an excellent book, *A Logbuilders Handbook*. In this book, Langsner describes in intimate detail the log hewing and log building method of Master Logsmith Peter Gott. When building his home, Gott hewed every timber from log and cut all the joinery with hand tools.

With such a labor-intensive method approach to building, it seems unlikely that Gott would be the one to revolutionize hewn log construction. Gott would saw kerfs into the logs and knock out the juggles. He would then rescore the log and hew away thin shavings, creating a flush surface.

As building requests increased, he found ways to lighten the labor involved. He soon learned that he could cut dovetail joints with incredible accuracy using a chain saw. He also noticed that since the Broadaxe only shaves a thin layer to create the hewn surface, the same effect could be had by purchasing logs sawn on two sides and lightly scoring and hewing off the sawn surface.

The fact that timbers can be hewn from either logs or dimensionally sawn material increases the income opportunities in hewing. On two different occasions neighbors have approached me with a need for a timber that exceeded the average carriage capacity of portable saw mills. In such a case, the ability to hew the log on the spot was the advantage. The man was able to get the dimension, the length, the wood that he wanted, and the result further enhanced the appearance of the house interior. In such a case, the skill I brought to the log clearly had value, enabling me to negotiate a price that I found reasonable.

If, on the other hand, a person wants hewn timbers primarily for the aesthetic value, it makes sense to purchase sawn material and hew off the sawn material. The customer must pay for the log and the labor of removing the bulk of the waste, along with the finish hewing of the timber. Whether the bulk waste is removed by sawmill or human sweat is irrelevant to the finished piece. It is a cost passed on to the customer. The hewing, however, is the skill that adds value to the product. This is where, above and beyond my costs, I figure the value of my labor and craft in setting the price.

As far as I can tell, there is only one company specializing in mail-order hand-hewn timbers. That company calls itself the Broad-Axe Beam Co. Their beams are 7 1/2" square, run in standard lengths from 8' to 16', are packaged in a cardboard sleeve, and shipped via common carrier. With such a business it becomes personal choice whether one wants to hew from log or re-hew a sawn timber. An arrangement could easily be made with a local mill, creating a fairly fixed cost for materials. Arrangements could also be established with a common carrier, so that shipping price could be accurately factored in. Keeping the customer options limited makes the response time quicker. One is not forced to hunt around for specific dimensional material.

If one combines hewing with skillful notch cutting and joinery, the value of one's labor increases dramatically.

Hewing as a trade has a long precedence. The British, very early in settling the colonies, sought skillful hewers for the ship-mast trade. Long, straight, massive white pines were carefully felled with axes. Prior to felling the giant, smaller pines were felled to act as a cushion for the mast tree. The entire length of the trunk, 3' to 6' diameter at the butt, 120' long, was taken from forest to water by oxen. From there it was

*Logs being measured and hewn into sixteen-sided ship masts in pre-revolutionary New England.*
*Drawing:* ***Ton Timber,*** *from* ***The King's Broad Arrow,*** *courtesy of Samuel F. Manning.*

*Square Timber Hewing. Archives of Ontario.*
*(Photo attributed to W. D. Watt, 1912-1913, Acc. 11778-4/S16944.)*

*Canadian hewers hewing timbers to be fastened into rafts.*
*The hewers are using Canada Pattern Broadaxes.*
*The one standing to the left is using a left-handed Broadaxe.*
(*Booth Camp Lumber Camp* around 1900, National Archives of Canada, C-075265.)

*A* ***cage de bois,*** *or squared timber raft, floating down river to port. This raft had a dining area and sleeping cabins.*
(*The Kitchen on a Raft,* National Archives of Canada, C-019892.)

floated, pulled by rowboat, to the mast yard. At the mast yard, each log was measured and hewn into a sixteen-sided, tapered mast.

The Napoleonic Wars opened one other trade venue for squared timbers. With Napoleon controlling Continental Europe, England looked toward its Canadian colony to supply its lumber needs. So began in earnest the square timber trade that was to last into the 20th century.

*Shantymen* would fell and hew pines into square timbers, some over forty feet long and two feet thick. The timbers were hauled by oxen over snow to water. In the spring giant rafts were made from the timbers, and the timber rafts were floated down river to the major ports, Quebec being a principal port. A timber raft could cover as much as seven acres of area. At port the rafts were disassembled and the timbers loaded aboard ships bound for England. The hewing trade was so vital to Ontario's economy that a hewer is depicted upon the Ontario provincial flag. A particular Broadaxe pattern, called the Canada pattern, was used in hewing, as was a special axe for scoring.

If one want to be a professional hewer, the expense for equipment would not be great. One would need, at minimum, a chain saw, $350, an axe, $30, and a Broadaxe, $80 to $250, depending upon make and type. In addition, one would probably need to purchase a drawknife, $50, a chalkline, a level, a tape measure, a pocketknife, and possibly one or two log dogs. For well less than $1000 all the tools necessary to establish a commercial hewing business could be purchased. I can think of few businesses that would require such a small output of capital.

The other two requirements are relative good health and hewing experience. Both would develop with the swinging of the axe.

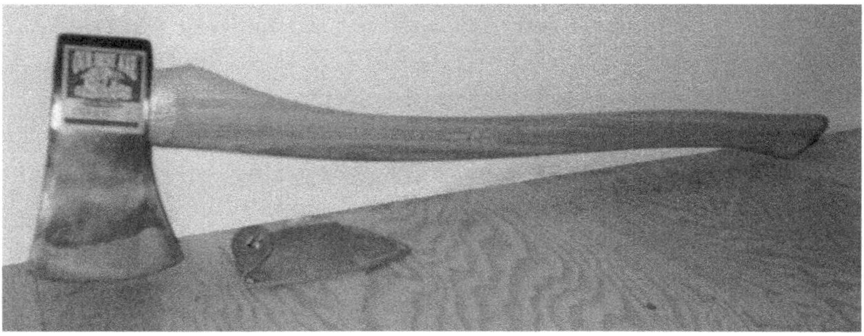

*A Snow and Nealley 3-1/2 lb. felling axe.*

# ACQUIRING AN AXE

*Near the end of March, 1845, I borrowed an axe. . . . It is difficult to begin without borrowing. But perhaps it is the most generous course thus to permit your fellow-men to have an interest in your enterprise. The owner of the axe, as he released his hold on it, said that it was the apple of his eye.*

—Henry David Thoreau, *Walden*

Most of us are not so fortunate, as was Odysseus, to have the goddess Calypso deliver an axe. We need to take some action on our part to acquire one. Before we can go out to acquire one, however, we need to define for ourselves exactly what we intend to do with the axe. Will it be used predominantly to split wood? to fell? to buck? to hew? Will it be used around home? Will it need to be sheathed? For example, the one-and-a-half-pound head of the Hudson Bay pattern axe with its three-and-a-half-inch bit and twenty-two-inch handle is the ideal camp axe, and, with a belt sheath, can easily be taken into the back country. To try, however, and fell large trees, square timbers, or build a cabin with such a small axe is an overwhelming task. On the other hand, to purchase a five- or six-pound bludgeon for felling trees may be more than we are conditioned to handle. The standard axe is generally a 2½-lb. to a 3½-lb. head with a 4" to 5" cutting bit and a 28" to 32" handle. If the axe is going to be used mostly for splitting firewood, I'd recommend an 8-lb. splitting maul, though a single-bit or poll axe would serve one well. The poll can be used to drive wooden wedges, called gluts, or the poll can be struck with a wooden club. If felling, bucking and hewing are the primary activities, then the double-bit axe cannot be beat. It is incredibly well balanced and has two cutting edges. Some people used to deliberately sharpen the two bits differently. One bit was sharpened for felling while the other was sharpened in a blunter, thicker fashion for limbing. This is a practice I have never used.

Perhaps it is the mystique of having been the tool of the burly, wool-shirted lumberjacks, but my double-bit axes are my pride and joy, the most enjoyable felling axes to use. They, also, are free of some of the abuses single-bit axes receive. Having no poll, the double-bit axe cannot be used to drive iron wedges, nor can it be struck with a steel hammer. It can only be used in the manner an axe was intended: to shape, dress, trim, chop, split, or sever. The double-bit axe has a reputation for being dangerous. When driven into a stump, a cutting surface remains exposed that could prove to be a serious hazard, should one trip or fall onto it. Some companies supply leather blade guards to help minimize hazard in storing or handling, but nothing but caution minimizes the risk while in the woods.

With few exceptions, axes are sold handled. Sometimes the handle the axe comes with detracts from what I envision would be its ideal use. I purchased a German Broadaxe with a $4^1/_2$-lb. head and a 32" handle. I found it was not my choice Broadaxe, but frequently I was in need of a Broad hatchet, which I did not have. I cut the handle of the Broadaxe very short and reshaped this stub of a handle to something I found functional. So at home was I with this Broad hatchet that I forgot it ever was

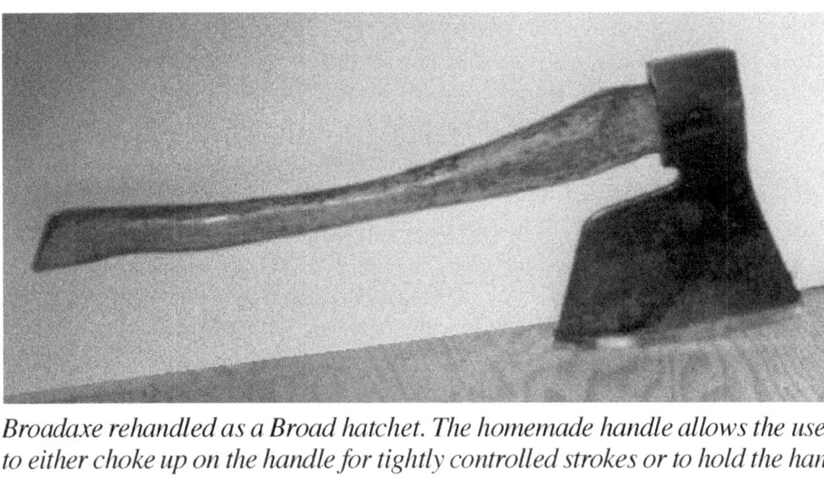

*Broadaxe rehandled as a Broad hatchet. The homemade handle allows the user to either choke up on the handle for tightly controlled strokes or to hold the handle at foot for more forceful rough work. The 18" long handle is long enough to allow one to use the tool as a two-handed Broadaxe if needed.*

*This 4-lb. axe with 32" handle is available for $100 from Lehman's at http://www.lehmans.com under the section* ***Timberframing.***

sold with a 32" handle until I recently saw it in the Lehman's catalog. With time I came to see the handle was a little too short. When working on precise work the short handle gave me excellent control, but I often wished the handle was slightly longer for more forceful, roughing out, as in the initial work of making an axe handle. I fashioned an 18" handle, with the wood thin enough to easily allow me to choke up on the handle. I also gave the handle a slight curve to add impact to my stroke. And when the job calls for it, I can still use the tool as a two-handed mini Broadaxe.

Even with a clear idea of what weight and pattern one wants, the issue of where to buy remains. Unless the axe is strictly for splitting firewood, department store chains should not be considered. They invariably have a tool department with an axe and maul hanging there, but we're looking for quality from a reputable manufacturer, something the department store purchaser may not. Some hardware stores, lumber yards and sporting-goods stores do have quality axes. Some do not. You need to look, ask and feel. Talk to people that have a reverence for axes and find out what manufacturers they recommend. If the store clerks know their stuff, they should be able to tell you why they have chosen to carry the particular axes they do. Mail order, whether through catalog or the Internet, is another option. Many mail-order companies pride themselves on quality, and the axes they carry simply have to meet their high standards. Purchase quality. A good axe takes an edge, keeps an edge, is balanced, made of quality steel, evenly tempered, and will give a lifetime's worth of work. An inferior axe may prove to be none of the above.

Obscure sources for axes are old-tool shops. Here one can frequently find several axes in need of handles. One may find a specialized axe that is far too costly or rare to purchase new. My Pennsylvania pattern Broadaxe was purchased from an old-tool shop, unhandled, for $35. Axes of this particular pattern are very expensive when purchased new. Cumberland General Store list a price of $230 for a Broadaxe of this pattern. To find one in good condition at this price was a real find. Or one may simply be looking for a utilitarian axe for splitting firewood. Before purchasing, check it over. If badly chipped, cracked or mushroomed, the bargain axe has been abused to the point of being a hazard but used need not be abused. Frequently one finds axe heads that appear as if they have never been handled and, indeed, that may be the case. Axe heads at one time were sold unhandled.

Unfortunately, bargains are bargains, and quality is quality, and the two frequently are not related. A good axe, such as those produced by Snow and Nealley, can still be purchased for forty dollars.

From time to time the quality of a particular axe manufacturer becomes widely renowned, and the axes created by this manufacturer become the standard by which all others are compared. In the last few years that manufacturer has been Gransfors Bruks. The easiest way to get information on the company, the axe making process, and the various axe patterns manufactured is to go to their web site at: http://www.gransfors.com.

Each Gransfors axe is handcrafted by an axesmith. The steel is heated and trip forged by the craftsman, as well as the shaping, tempering, grinding and honing. In addition to stamping the Gransfors's logo on the axe, the craftsman stamps his/her initials onto the axe. Each axe becomes a statement of the craftsmanship of the axesmith. Several companies are currently selling Gransfors axes, though not every company is selling the entire line. An easy way to locate mail-order companies selling Gransfors axes is simply to type in "Gransfors Bruks axes" in the search box of an internet search engine and several retailers will appear. Gransfors Bruks axes are fairly expensive, but the quality Swedish steel and excellent craftsmanship have a cost. The prices do vary widely from retailer to retailer. One wishing to purchase a Gransfors' axe would do well to browse through several of the sites. The Swedish Broadaxe had prices varying from $130 to $200. Felling axes and splitting mauls averaged two times what one would expect to pay for comparable items from a reputable American company, as much as three or four times what one would expect to pay from a generic, mass-producing axe manufacturer such as Collins or Woodings-Verona. Each Gransfors Bruks axe comes with a book on the maintenance and use of axes.

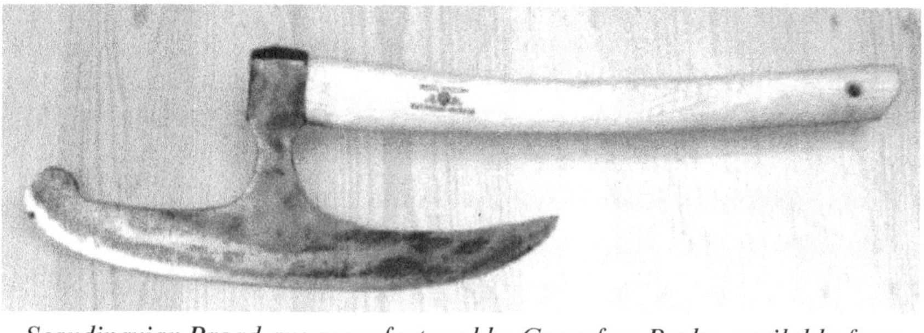

*Scandinavian Broad axe manufactured by Gransfors Bruks, available from Dieter Schmidt Feine Werkzeuge at http://www.fine-tools.com*

Gransfors produces several unique and unusual patterns. Perhaps the most unusual is an axe they call the "Scandinavian Broadaxe." This is, by all appearances, a copy of an ancient T-axe, and Gransfors is the only manufacturer I know making such an axe.

Another Swedish manufacturer is S A Wetterling. Like Gransfors, they produce mostly axes following traditional Swedish patterns rather than American patterns. These axes are hand-forged of Swedish Steel, using a special steel alloy involving iron, carbon, silicon, manganese and vanadium. The company claims the alloy makes quality hardening possible with a hardness of 57-58. Their Broadaxe is a fine working tool, double-beveled with an eight-inch bit and a 26" handle. Like Gransfors, only the bit is polished. The axe is available at www.mudpond.net for $105. This is perhaps one of the finest buys available for one wishing to purchase a Swedish Broadaxe.

A third Swedish manufacturer with a longer history than either Gransfors or S A Wetterling is Hults Bruk with the trade name AGDOR. Hults has its roots going back to a 1697 forge. It is the oldest manufacturer of axes in Northern Europe. It is a major toolmaker in the world today, though strangely not well known in the United States. One of the

*A double-bit axe manufactured by Hults Bruk. Perhaps no axe has been used by the author as much as this axe. It comes beautifully polished, wonderfully balanced and evenly tempered. This axe takes a fine edge and keeps it. I've been using it since 1982.*

few North American suppliers that I could find was Northdoorway Homestead Outfitters at: http://northdoorway.com/farmgarden/fellingaxe.htm.

Northdoorway sells three models of AGDOR axes: a 2½-lb. axe with a 28" handle ($25), a 3½-lb. axe with a 36" handle ($36), and the world renowned Arvika Five-Star Racing Axe with its 4½-lb. fully polished head and 32" handle. The Racing Axe was originally designed for working hardwood but its reputation has grown, making it a popular favorite in world chopping competitions. I received, as a Christmas gift, a Hults double-bit axe, purchased from Smith and Hawken, back in 1982. Allen Klenman, author of the book *Axe Makers of North America,* says of AGDOR, "When you buy AGDOR, you can buy no better axe." My years of using the double bit have convinced me Klenman is right.

I have spoken enough about Snow and Nealley quality. Snow and Nealley has narrowed its marketing focus in the last few years. 70% of Snow and Nealley's sales now come from garden tools. Only thirty percent is currently from axes and mauls. Of this thirty percent, a growing proportion is the Hudson Bay pattern kindling axe. They continue to manufacture a quality line. Axe collectors are attracted to the double-bit axes, which with the 36" handle are impressive-looking tools.

Perhaps the easiest way to purchase a Snow and Nealley axe is to purchase directly from the company. The Web address is http://www.snowandnealley.com. The axes are no longer drop forged at the Bangor manufacturing site, but the axes are still ground, heat tempered, and honed at the manufacturing site. The craftsmen can be observed working from the showroom, grinding the bevel and removing the rough edges from drop forging. One can also observe the axe cutting edge being heated to an orange glow in the tempering oven. The craftsman removes the axe with tongs and quenches the axe in a brine-filled tub, placing it on the rack to receive its finished edge and handle.

*Snow and Nealley double-bit axe with 36" handle.*

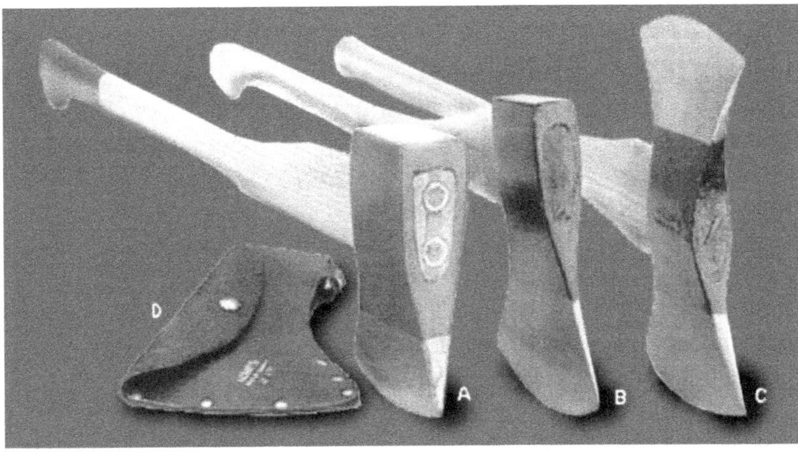


*Patterns of Iltis Ox-Head axes sold by Lee Valley Tools (above). Tuatahi Competition Chopping axe with 31½" handle, available from Baileys for approximately $300, www.bailysonline.com (below).*

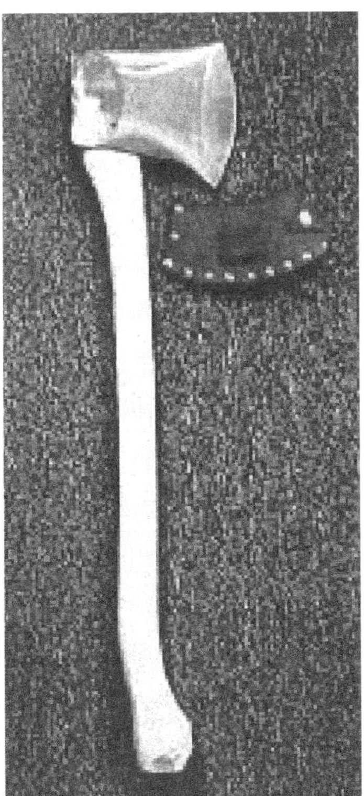

For those preferring German axes, Lee Valley Tools sells Iltis Ox-Head axes.

Lee Valley says of this axe, "The Iltis felling axe, the best woodsman's axe available anywhere, is designed for felling, limbing and notching. The slim profile design (2" back of the face, the blade is only ¼" thick) gives excellent penetration by minimizing the wedging action. The precise forging and tempering result in steel that rings like a bell."[24] The single-bit felling axe is priced around $55 and the double-bit is $75.

If what you truly want is an Australian Racing Axe designed strictly for axemen competitions, the axe to purchase is the Tuatahi Competition Chopping Axe.

As we move further away from individualized craftsmanship and to mass-produced, we find Collins Axes. Collins has been in the axe-making business since 1826. Unlike Gransfors Bruks, that has sought to keep production limited in order to preserve the highest standards of quality, Collins has sought the mass-market. Collins axes can be found in basically every state. Home Depot carries Collins axes and replacement handles almost exclusively. Collins drop-forges its axes from high-carbon steel. The axes are hand-ground, and heat-treated. The standard of quality, however, is not that of the axes listed above. The tools are ground coarsely, especially the splitting mauls. By mass-marketing its axes and mauls, Collins is forced to find cost cutting steps. The fine polish, tempering or honing that one would receive in a more expensive axe is not present in a Collins axe.

Collins axes come with either a hickory or fiberglass handle. Home Depot sells both styles. The most common pattern sold is the Michigan pattern, 3½-lb. axe. Fiberglass-handled axes are a few dollars more expensive than the Hickory-handled axes. At Home Depot, the Hickory-handled Michigan pattern axe costs about $20.

In addition to the above, Collins has created another line called the Black Knight axes. What separates this line from the others is the manner in which the handle is held to the axe. Rather than relying on steel or wood wedges, or epoxy to hold the axe, the axe is held to the handle by means of a plastic sleeve. The sleeve also doubles as a handle guard. I have never used one of these axes or mauls, so I cannot tell you how secure the axe is to the handle. Unlike conventional handles, the handle protrudes beyond the axe head. The current system uses the same handle for both axe and maul. This means that one must accept a straight handle for the axe. And the axe eye must be wider than a conventional axe eye, making the axe seem bulkier, more maul-like than axe-like. The Black Knight line appears to be useful primarily for splitting firewood, less useful for chopping or hewing. The new handle design reduces the labor involved in fitting a handle. The axe or maul can simply be press-fitted. Putting in a replacement handle appears equally simple. The handles come in wood or fiberglass.

To visit the Collins Web site go to http://www.mannedge.com.collins.htm. The site gives the history of Collins axes, shows the manufacturing process, and shows examples of the axes manufactured. In addition, the site offers useful information to axe users, such as how to sharpen an axe, how to replace a handle, either conventional or Black Knight, common abuses to avoid, and how to use axes or mauls.

Another mass-marketing manufacturer of axes and mauls is Woodings-Verona. WalMart and many chain hardware stores carry this line. Generally, if a store carries Collins axes, it is not likely to carry Woodings-Verona. These two are in direct competition for the same market. These are generic quality axes and mauls that can be purchased for around $20. I purchased a Woodings-Verona splitting maul from Walmart several years ago. The handle was thicker than normal. At first I thought having a thicker handle would be a plus. The fatter handle appears to have taken its toll upon my right elbow. After purchasing a Snow and Nealley maul with its more streamlined handle, I noticed the discomfort in my right elbow subsided.

I have been trying to explain to myself the difference between the two mauls. Both my Snow and Nealley maul and my Woodings-Verona maul are eight-pound mauls. Both have wood handles. Both appear much the same. But for reasons I cannot decipher, the Snow and Nealley maul works much easier. This was shown to me a few years back when a few of us were at a friend's house, helping him split firewood. Mike Shannon seemed to be effortlessly splitting wood with his Snow and Nealley maul while I struggled with my Woodings-Verona maul. I thought maybe it was his swinging style, but I could see little difference. We swapped mauls for a while and I instantly experienced the difference. With the Snow and Nealley maul it felt as if my swings were effortless. Gravity alone appeared to be doing the work.

This analysis is very unscientific. I cannot tell you why one appeared to work better than the other. Perhaps, in actuality, they worked equally well. Perhaps the only real difference is that the Snow and Nealley handle fits my hands better. The head of the Snow and Nealley maul is slightly more polished and a bit more streamlined. I also noticed the handle protrudes from the maul at a slightly different angle. Just picking up the Snow and Nealley maul, it feels better balanced than the Woodings-Verona maul.

I split a lot of wood with the Woodings-Verona maul. It still has the original handle in it and I am certain I could split wood with it for the rest of my life. It was purchased at less than half the price of a Snow and Nealley maul. The head is not pitted; it takes and keeps an edge fairly well. I cannot justify complaining about Woodings-Verona's splitting maul.

Being a traditionalist, I have never used a fiberglass handle. I prefer wood handles and can give no reason for my preference other than it is organic in nature and something I can create and shape myself.

To visit the Woodings-Verona website go to http://www.woodings verona.

To purchase a Broadaxe, one will have to leave the department stores and general hardware stores behind. Mail order catalogs or online retailers are practically the only way to purchase a Broadaxe. Currently, the least-expensive Broadaxe on the market is the Woodcraft Supply Kent Hewing Axe. If one lives near one of the Woodcraft's outlets it is possible to purchase the axe directly. If not, the axe would have to be purchased by phone or by Internet. Woodcraft Supply also sells froes. The web address is http://www.woodcraft.com. The current price is $60 for the axe, sold unhandled, and $20 for the handle. This is still $20 less than the price Lehman's charges for its Broadaxe (http://www.lehmans.com). Lehman's Broadaxe, however, is German made.

An exceptional site for axes is Dieter Schmidt Feine Werkzeuge at http://www.fine-tools.com. Not only does Deiter Schmidt sell the basic line of Gransfors Bruks axes, it sells a few Gransfors' axes available at few other sites. One is the model 1700 Joiners axe.

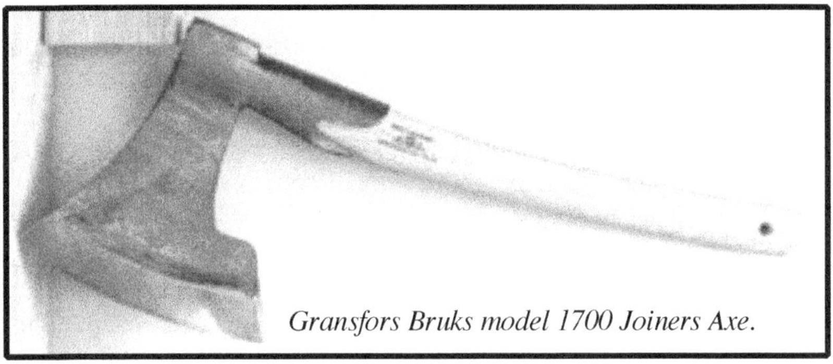

*Gransfors Bruks model 1700 Joiners Axe.*

This is a very pricey axe (over $350), but it is a functional work of art.

Another exceptional axe sold by Schmidt is the Austrian Broadaxe manufactured by Muller. Again we are talking about a $350 axe, but for an axe collector such as me, these two axes appear almost irresistible.

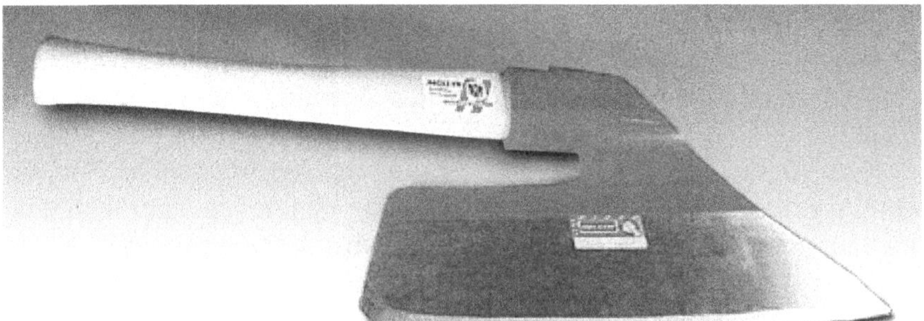

*Muller's Austrian Bearded Broadaxe.*

Two very useful sights are Lee Valley Tools, http://www.leevalley.com and Schroeder's Log Home Supply, http://www.loghelp.com. Both are good sources for Gransfors Bruks axes, both sell accessories such as Peaveys, Canthooks, timber carriers, bark spuds, log dogs and froes. Schroeder sells the model 1700 Gransfors' joiners axe, but no

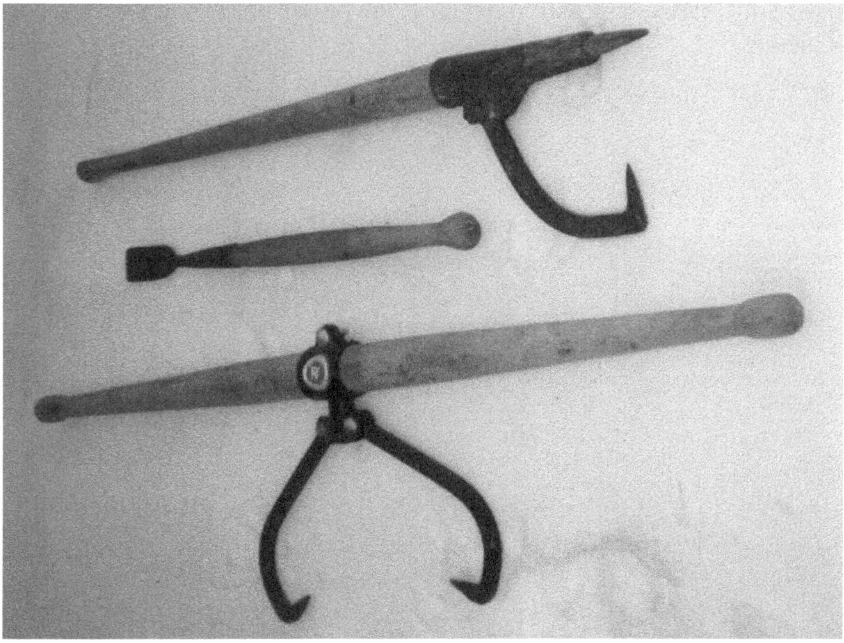

*Helpful Accessories: top—Peavey; middle—Bark Spud; bottom—Timber Carrier. These are available from Peavey Manufacturing; www.peaveymfg.com.*

price is listed. To request a price, one would have to contact Schroeders directly.

If one wishes to purchase tomahawks or other small reproductions, simply type Tomahawk into the search box of any search engine and several sites should appear. Some of these appear quite functional and most are priced reasonably. Three Web addresses for Tomahawks are: http://www.tuscanytrading.com,

http://www.duckhunter77.com, and http://tradingpage.com.

I am aware there are axe manufacturers that I have not listed. My intention was simply to make others aware of some of the variety and differences in quality and styles of axes available, and to help connect people to possible sources of axes. The number of axes one really needs is rather limited. For many of us that number is one. And if one axe is all that is needed, and one wishes to experience joy when using it, that axe must meet one's needs and respond as expected when used. A word of caution: as one learns the intricacies of axemanship, an addictive drive to possess and use a variety of axes out there on the market may seize one's soul, leading one to desire the rarest and most expensive of axes. Unfortunately, many remain out of my economic reach. Ah! but someday . . .

*The author's pine lot*

# WOODLAND STEWARDSHIP AND THE AXE

*My days in the woods were not very long ones; yet I usually carried my dinner of bread and butter, and read the newspaper in which it was wrapped, at noon, sitting amid the green pine boughs which I had cut off, and to my bread was imparted some of its fragrance, for my hands were covered with a thick coat of pitch. Before I had done I was more the friend than the foe of the pine tree, though I had cut down some of them, having become better acquainted with it.*

—Henry David Thoreau, *Walden.*

I have spoken of felling, cutting, splitting, hewing and building. One could easily get the impression that my woodlot is a disfigured mess, but that is not the case at all. I was fortunate enough to purchase a pine lot so dense and choked that it begged to be thinned. Young dead pines fueled my sugar stove and kindled fires in my home for years. The pines felled for the house were always thinnings, saving the best trees for some future stretching well beyond the day I am lowered into the earth. With a pole saw, the pines were limbed as high as I could reach. The only land I really cleared was an abandoned field choked with pin cherry, poplar and alder. Here the alders were cut and stacked, the land fenced, and goats and sheep introduced, bringing the land back to green meadow.

For a quarter of a century my woodlot has provided me with logs, beams, poles, shakes, fence posts, firewood, balsam-wreath brush, and maple syrup. I have not, however, depleted the supply of any of the above, and the straightest, tallest trees remain. If one walked my woodlot one would be apt to say that I have cut too little, not too much. I have but 12 acres of land, only 9 of which are woods, yet there are sections of these 9 acres in which I have never even felled a single tree.

When one's woodlot supplies so many of one's necessities, one spends considerable time in the woodlot working it. The woodlot becomes like a perennial garden. I find myself grooming the lot, weeding and harvesting. The woodlot, itself, becomes as much the finished product as the timber I am hewing or the firewood I am splitting. And sometimes, like a horrible blight, powerful winds or heavy ice storms pass through the woodlot, wreaking heavy destruction. At such times I become discouraged, thinking all my work in vain, wondering if the woodlot can be saved. Little by little the woods are cleaned, firewood stacked, timbers salvaged, brush piled. The trees throw out new limbs, filling out the gaping holes in the canopy. With time I forget the destructive forces ever passed.

It is not that the woodlot steward works against nature, but neither is it correct to say that the steward simply lets nature take its course. It is a collaborative dance where sometimes the steward trips and stumbles, having misread the partner; but other times it is a collaborative harmony. The small maple sapling that was given growing room years ago is now reaching high into the canopy and has enough girth to be tapped for sugar. Pines are felled to open the canopy and a few years later the canopy is again closed, but the pines stand fuller, broader than they used to be.

In theory, a sustainable rate of harvest is one cord of wood per acre. But in reality, the initial cut in a long-ignored or abused woodlot may be as high as 2 or 3 cords per acre. To begin any kind of woodland management, simply take a walk around and through the woodlot, taking a mental inventory of what is there. One section may be predominantly hardwood, another area thick with pine, and another an overstory of hardwood crowded by an understory of softwood. The soil, slope and drainage have a lot to do with what trees grow where, so even small woodlots experience marked differences in tree species growing in one section compared with those in another section but a hundred feet away.

With the inventory complete, develop some goals for the woodlot. Perhaps the goal is a sugar bush, or to raise veneer or high-grade lumber. Even if we have no intention of ever harvesting these most valuable trees in our woodlot, clarifying the goals keeps us honest and makes apparent which trees need to be thinned or culled.

A young stand of trees starts with 4000 to 6000 stems per acre. At maturity (20" in diameter), less than one hundred trees per acre will sur-

*Before thinning*

*After thinning.*

*Photos from* ***Agriculture for Beginners,*** *1914, pp. 233-235.*

vive. A mature sugar bush with trees 30" to 48" in diameter will be less than thirty-five trees per acre. As the woodland slowly matures, one may either let natural selection decide which trees will survive and which ones will die, or one can take part in the process by thinning and cutting selectively so that a young straight and vigorous bole will not die due to being overshadowed by fast growing, short-lived, inferior species such as poplar, or crowded out by crooked, diseased or forked trees that should be culled.

One hundred trees per acre assumes these mature trees are spaced roughly twenty feet apart. Using this assumption, the crop trees one intends to foster must likewise be twenty feet apart, and what is between them will *gradually* be removed over the years to give the crop trees crown space. If everything between the crop trees were removed all at once, sunscald, ice and wind damage would destroy many of these young trees.

*Thinning the pines supplied me with all the building logs and shingle bolts I needed.*

The proper way to thin is to remove one to three trees from around a crop tree, opening three to four feet of crown space on at least two sides. If a large tree is removed, that crown space will be considerably greater than three to four feet, perhaps closer to twelve to fifteen feet. No more thinning need be done around this tree until the canopy again closes, at which time the crown space must be opened by felling one to three trees.

Naturally, if the desired goal is a sugar bush, the Sugar Maple is given preference over other trees when selecting crop trees. Diversity, however, in the woodlot is a defense against diseases that could thrive on a monoculture woodlot. Some species, such as Balsam Fir, are short-lived, prone to heart rot, and choke out quality hardwoods if left uncontrolled. Such trees make poor crop trees.

When working in the woodlot, it is a good idea to have in mind the potential inherent in the log. One may be cutting firewood, but a knotless, 8"-thick piece of White Ash could yield several good handles. Often when I am felling pines for building timber, I cut out clear eighteen-inch sections for shake material out of what would have been waste material. The remaining waste is cut into firewood. Sometimes out of the tops I cut out a fence post or two, pointing them right there in the woods. The remaining limbs and brush that are too small for the cookstove are piled neatly. Often times in the spring, while boiling maple sap, I return even to these "brush" piles and salvage dry wood for the sap stove.

*One 24' log and 3 shingle bolts were taken from this tree. The remainder was cut into fuelwood.*

If one fells a tree, perhaps the model for utilization of that tree comes from the coniferous belt of Europe, where forests have been under cultivation for centuries.

*Almost complete utilization, as found in a typical logging scene in Norway spruce in Germany [early twentieth century]. The larger trees are cut into saw logs. The top logs and the smaller trees are cut into pulpwood. All logs are stripped of bark, which is used for tanning purposes. The stumps are cut low, the top branches and small pieces corded and stacked for fuel wood. Even the smallest limbs and branches are utilized. Later, the stumps are grubbed out and converted into charcoal.*

*Photo from* ***Elements of Forestry,*** *1929 p. 13.*

On my particular woodlot, firewood is a major concern. Wood is my principal source of heat and winters are long. Firewood in and of itself requires no plan other than having the woodlot sustain itself so that enough wood can be removed each year to meet my heating needs. Though, when all my other wood needs and concerns are factored in, management becomes a more complex issue. Firewood is diseased or broken trees, inferior species, or trees that are crowding desirable tree species. Though I desire sufficient quantities of good heating hardwood in my woodshed, softwood tops and culls comprise a good portion of the wood I burn. Yet I only cull and thin until my wood needs are met for the year. I must be honest, however, some years I do not even find enough time to meet my wood needs. If my wood needs are met, even if other parts of the woodlot could benefit from thinning, they must wait until fuelwood or building-pole needs dictate that I cut. But if I see an accumulation of pines that need serious thinning, it isn't long before I decide I need a new building project.

To use an axe does not have to be an act of environmental abuse. In a world of diminishing resources one has the opportunity, with minimal tools and/or skills, to build a simple home from woodlot thinnings, heated with fuel from culled trees. One's life becomes an environmental statement of frugal simplicity.

*An environmental statement:*
*a house built of pine thinnings heated with culled firewood.*

*Frost Powder House built in Eliot, Maine in 1734. Hewn log construction involv - ing dovetail joinery has been in use in New Hampshire and Maine since the late 17th century.*

# THE BASICS OF HEWN-LOG CABIN BUILDING

*There is no building which fits so naturally in a wild landscape as a good old-fashioned log cabin . . .*

*When I make the claim that any ordinary man can build himself a summer home, I do not mean to say that he will not make blunders and plenty of them; only fools never make mistakes, wise men profit by them, and the reader may profit by mine, for there is no lack of them in our log house at Big Tink. But the house still stands on the bank overlooking the lake and is practically as sound as it was when the last spike was driven, twenty seven years ago.*

—D. C. Beard, *Shelters, Shacks and Shanties*

I have spoken much about hand-hewing timbers and the historical connection of axes and log structures. Though my focus throughout this work has been the axe and its use, I now diverge from that focus. Rather than writing about how the axe shapes wood, this chapter is concerned with how to join axe-shaped timbers to create a log structure.

Though hewn timbers can be used in post and beam frames as well as log structures, the joinery involved in cutting and raising a post-and-beam frame are varied and complex and beyond the scope of this work. If you have hewn timbers with the express intent of raising such a structure, my recommendation is to purchase a good timber frame book.

Log structures, on the other hand, may require more joint cutting than a timber frame but the joinery is repetitive and simpler than with a post and beam frame, and far less critical. A sloppy corner joint may cause draft problems, but it does not threaten the integrity of the entire structure. Only three joints are necessary to build the hewn log cabin: the Half-Dovetail joint for the wall logs, pocket mortises for the floor joists, and the Birdsmouth for the rafters. Of these three, only the Birdsmouth is difficult, and many a cabin builder dispenses with this joint altogether, relying rather upon a barely notched rafter and a heavy spike or peg.

Before cutting any joinery, it is important that the log is cut to proper length and the ends are square and true. When hewing in the woods, I generally cut the logs longer than is needed for the building, with the intent that I will cut the ends square at the building site. When cutting the ends of a log, I use a framing square held against the length of the log and draw my lines. At minimum two sides must be marked. It is even better if three are marked.

To simply draw one line and try to cut the end square with the rest of the log is chance. With only a line drawn across the top there is no reference that the cut on the vertical is true and square to the log.

With the logs cut square and to length, the sills can be placed. Whether the cabin is set upon a foundation wall, concrete piers, or merely resting upon rocks or concrete blocks, the builder will have to set floor joists for the principle floor and floor joists for the second floor if the cabin has one. The best way by far is to cut pockets into the sills and

*To cut the end square, use a framing square held against the length of log. Mark two sides, this gives the plane the saw must follow.*

set the floor joists into these pockets. Again, as with every log, the floor joists must have their ends cut square and true if they are to properly fit into the joist pockets.

*Floor joists set into carrying timber*

I generally place the floor joist 2 foot on center. The mortise pockets penetrate the beam two inches deep and extend as far down as is necessary to accept the entire floor joist. At least two inches of uncut wood must be left to the sill beneath the joist. That sometimes means the joist must be trimmed. For example, if the sill is eight inches wide, but the joist is seven inches in width, the bottom of the floor joist, where it is to enter the beam, must have one inch of wood shaved from its underside.

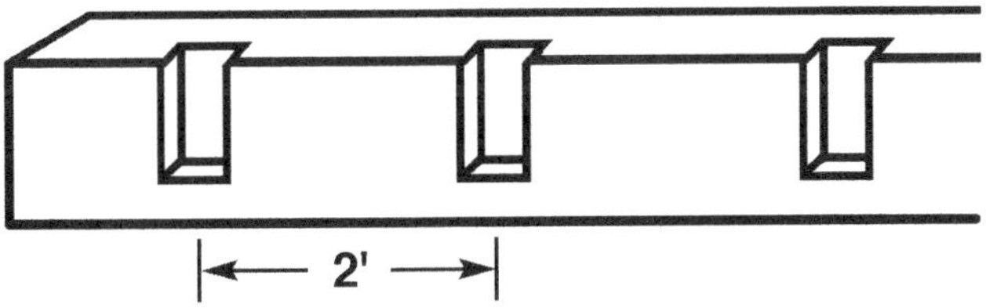


To layout the joist pockets onto a timber, establish chalklines. If the joists are to penetrate two inches into the sill, measure two inches from the edge at each end of the sill and snap a chalkline connecting these two points. If the joist is to drop six inches down into the sill, mark the measurements and snap the line. This will aid in keeping all joists even once the pockets are cut. Mark out the joist mortises using a framing square. Once all the joist pockets are marked, use a circular saw or chain saw to carefully cut into the sill along the lines established. When using a chain saw to cut joinery, we have to exercise special care. The chain saw, when sharp, is capable of cutting with incredible speed. In the woods, the woodcutter lets gravity simply pull the saw through the log. When cutting joinery, forget letting gravity do the work or your piece will be ruined. The saw must be spinning before the cut is begun, therefore incredible accuracy is required in order that the saw hits the line, and the saw must be held back, allowing it to cut a slow, controlled cut. If care and caution are used, the saw is very accurate. It will cut where you put it and to the depth that you allow it. If the cutting ends out sloppy, your own carelessness will be the only reason. If you have never cut joinery with a chain saw, I recommend you practice with scraps until you are familiar enough with how to approach the cut, control the cut and restrain the saw from over-cutting. It would be a shame to damage a well hewn log through poor skill with the chain saw.

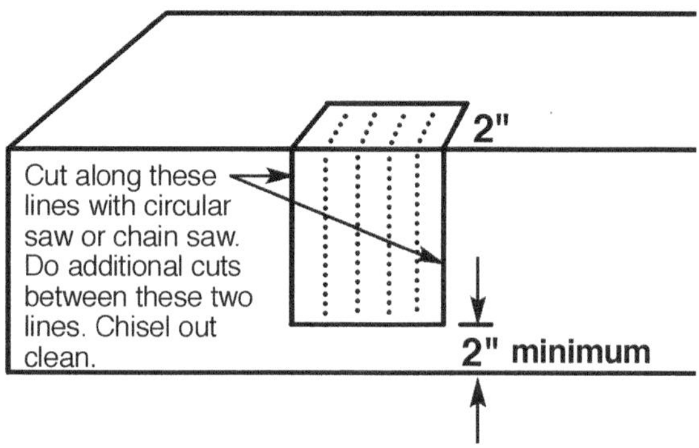


Once the sills and floor joists are in place, the walls can be raised. The half-dovetail joint works well with hewn logs. The joint naturally drains, preventing the logs from rotting due to moisture buildup. The

*Joist pocket being cut out with a chain saw. Care must be taken not to cut too deep either into the thickness or width of the log.*

joint is self-locking, helping to pull the cabin together and hold it together without the use of either pegs or nails. And the joint is fairly easy to cut. It can be done with no other tools than a chain saw or a handsaw and axe.

*Waste wood is then cleaned out with a chisel.*

*The joist may have to have the bottom undercut to fit the mortise pocket. This is easily done by cutting the vertical cut with a saw and hewing the horizontal line with the hewing axe.*

*The fitted floor joist*

I hew my logs down to a uniform thickness of six inches. Others may prefer to keep the logs eight inches thick. The thickness of the logs does not matter. What does matter is that all the logs have a uniform thickness. In addition to keeping uniformly straight walls inside and out, it makes cutting the joinery much easier. I use a two-inch drop for convenience. There is, as far as I know, no definite rule that says a joint must have a specific slope. The reason I use the two inch drop is because that is the width of a standard carpenter's framing square. The framing square can be placed upon the timber. The high point will be where the top of the framing square intersects the inside edge of the joint, and the bottom mark will be where the bottom of the framing square intersects the outside edge of the joint.

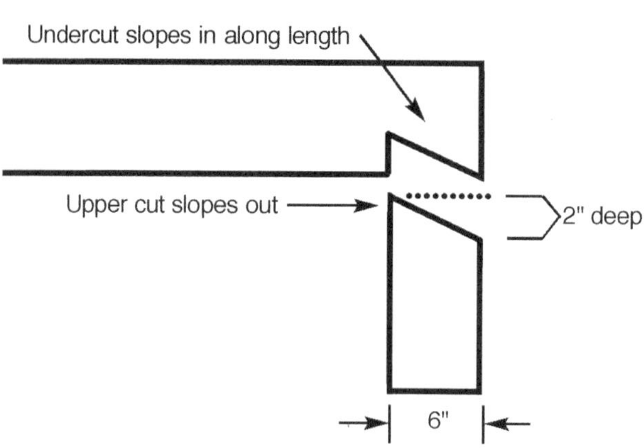


*The two cuts are a match: six inches long with a two-inch drop. They fit one into the other, locking the joint.*

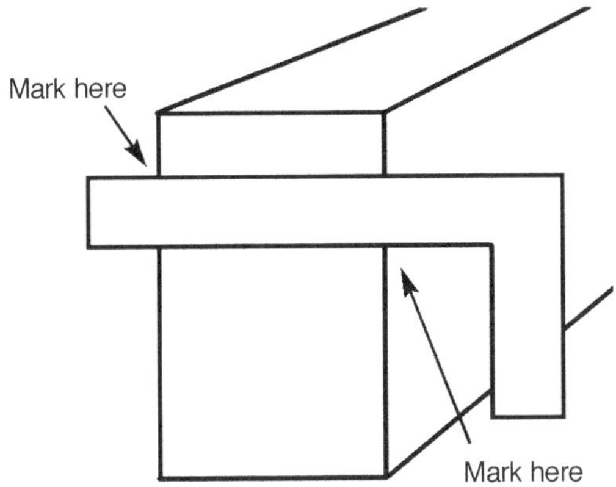


*Using a framing square to mark out top portion of half-dovetail joint.*

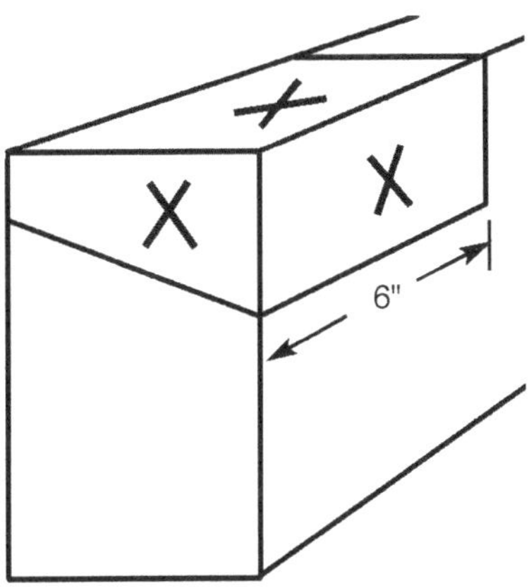


*Connect the two marks and extend line back six inches. The area marked with X is the wood that will be removed.*

The lower portion of the half-dovetail joint can likewise be drawn using the framing square.

Synthetic chinking is perhaps the most expensive material I purchase for a cabin. There are other options for chinking a cabin, but, at least for the outside of the cabin, I find these other options problematic, especially when applied incorrectly. I speak from experience. Water working in behind cement mortar chinking almost rotted one of my logs. The chinking was removed. The log had to have a portion of its surface hewn and chiseled to remove the fungi-decayed wood, and the chinking was replaced with synthetic chinking (which holds to the log better), keeping water from working in behind it.

To keep the chinking spaces minimal, I find it necessary to measure and set the joint into the log deep enough so that only a very small space remains between the logs along the length of the wall. Be careful, however, not to set the joint too deep into the log. In such an instance, the logs along the length may actually be resting upon one another, but a space may lie between the logs at the dovetail joint, decreasing its ability to lock the walls. When logs are generally uniform, having no more than a 2" difference in height, variance in depth is minimal.

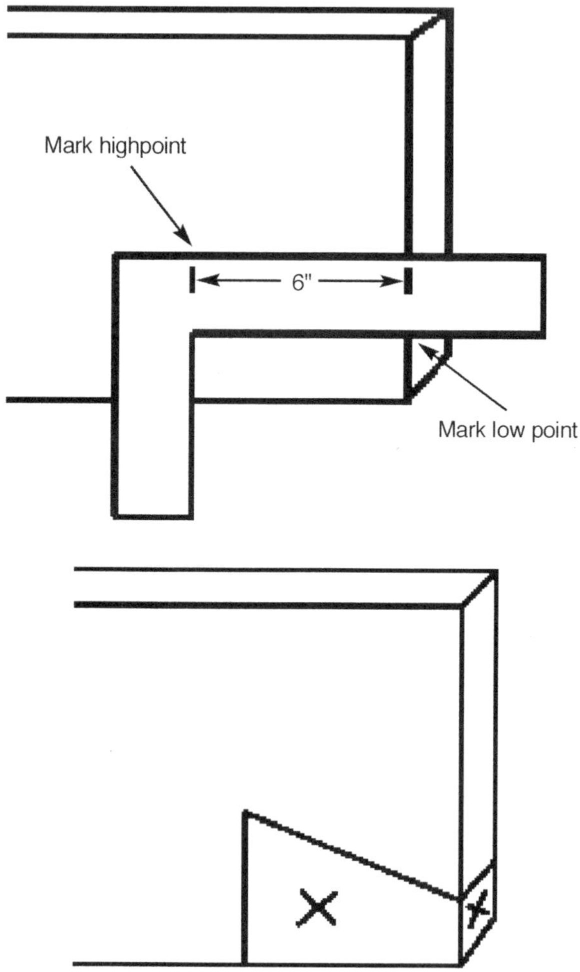


*Connect the two marks and extend the lines. A framing square should be used to mark both sides on the bottom portion of half-dovetail. X indicates the wood to be removed.*

The following photographs demonstrate the process of cutting the half-dovetail joint.

*The depth of the joint is cut so the logs rest upon one another without causing the joint to float. The depth into the log that the joint may have to be recessed varies and in some instances can be quite considerable, especially when logs 12" high are used with logs 8" high as shown by the log third from top left.*

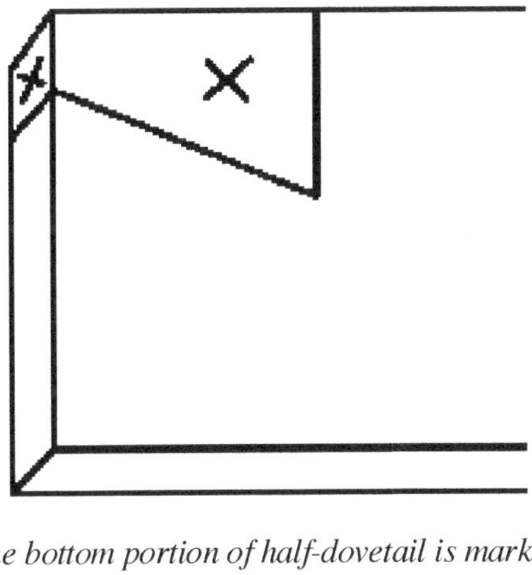

*The bottom portion of half-dovetail is marked.*

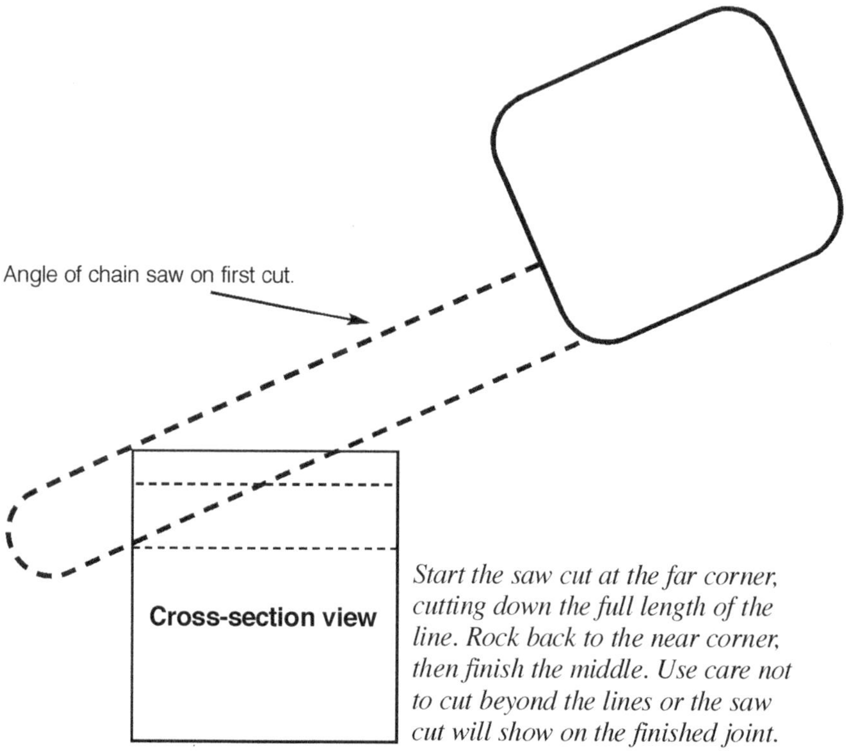


*Start the saw cut at the far corner, cutting down the full length of the line. Rock back to the near corner, then finish the middle. Use care not to cut beyond the lines or the saw cut will show on the finished joint.*

*Roll the log onto its side, then hew out the waste with your axe. The first few axe blows remove the bulk of the waste; then carefully hew to the line.*

*If your prefer to cut out waste with a saw rather than by hewing, do not allow the saw to go beyond your pencil lines.*

*Chisel the corner clean, along with any high points or irregularities. Chiseling the corner is especially important when using a chain saw, which leaves corners irregular and rough.*

*Now, mark and cut out the other side as described. If, upon placing the logs, there is a discrepancy in the fit, scribe the variance onto the top log and hew to the new line. If the joint was cut too deep and the top log is floating at the joint, remove the log and hew the underside of the top log until the joint sits tight.*

If my methodology appears too simplistic, a more mathematical and involved approach is taken by Drew Langsner in *A Logbuilder's Handbook.*

Door and window openings must be cut plumb. These can be cut as the walls are raised or after the walls are raised, depending upon personal preference. If 6"-thick walls are used, commercially available 2" by 6" planks can be used to frame the door and window openings.

When the walls reach the desired height, the top logs, or plates as they are called, are placed upon the walls. The plates carry the roof rafters. Because of the outward thrust of the roof, the plates should be secured at the corners with either lagbolts or trunnels (wooden pins). In traditional hewn-cabin construction, joining the rafters and attaching the rafters to the plates involves the most difficult joinery. There are, however, other options for those who have neither the desire to learn such joinery nor the time involved in cutting the joinery. Regardless of what manner of fitting rafters is used, one still must calculate roof angle and rafter length. To do so requires some basic Math skills and the use of the Pythagorean theorem — $a^2 + b^2 = c^2$. In this case, we use Half the Width of the Cabin$^2$ + The Roof Height$^2$ to give us the Rafter Length$^2$.

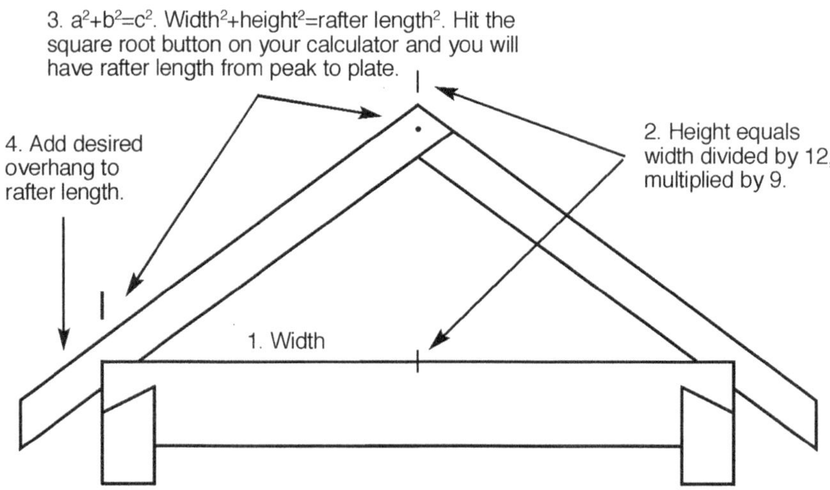


*Calculating Rafter Length.*

Measuring the width of the cabin from outside edge to midpoint is simple and basic. Calculating the height of the roof is equally simple and based upon the width of the cabin. The above illustration is based upon the fact that the roof will be a 9:12 pitch, meaning that for every foot in width, the roof will rise 9" in height. If the roof were a 12:12 pitch, the height would be the same as the width. To calculate height, decide upon the roof pitch, divide half the width of the cabin by 12 and multiply by the desired pitch, whether it be a 4-pitch, 9-pitch or 12-pitch. Plug these numbers into the Pythagorean theorem, hit the square root button on the calculator and you have the rafter length from plate to peak. Add to this length any desired overhang and you have the rafter length.

Once the roof pitch is determined and the rafter length calculated it is possible, using a framing square, to cut the rafters.

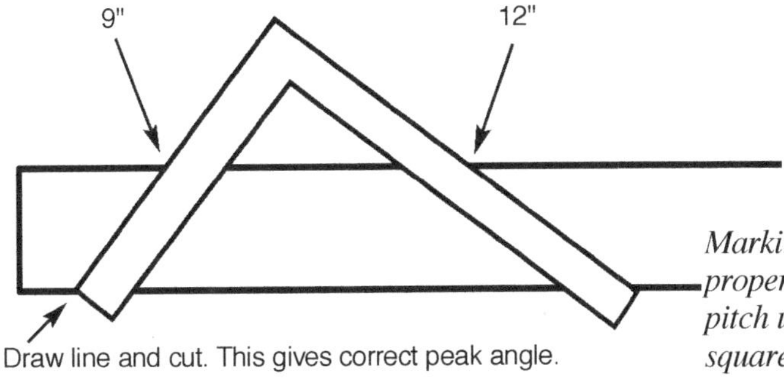


*Marking rafters at proper angle for 9:12 pitch using a framing square.*

The illustration above demonstrates how the peak angle is determined. If the roof pitch is 4:12 instead of 9:12, the framing square would be set to intersect the beam at 4 inches and 12 inches rather than at 9 inches and 12 inches as the illustration shows.

*A simple way to join rafters: simply butt against a ridge board and nail.*

A very simple option for joining rafters at the peak is simply to butt them against a ridge board.

The ridge board is temporarily braced into place. The rafters are butted against it and nailed. Once the rafters are up, the temporary bracing holding the ridge board no longer serves any function and can be removed.

Another simple method for joining rafters at the peak is to rest the rafters upon a ridge beam and simply butt the rafters to one another. This is an easy and effective method when working alone with heavy, hewn rafters. It also provides additional support for the roof, particularly when the roof has a shallow pitch.

*Rafter butt joined, supported by a carrying timber.*

In both of the above examples, the rafters are used with the point of the rafters facing up.

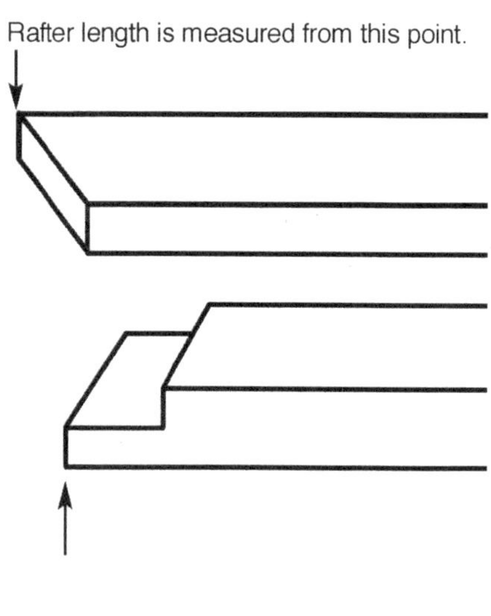


If, however, one prefers a traditional approach to rafter joinery, the rafters should be lap-joined and pegged. When rafters are lap-joined or mortised and tenoned, the rafter is used in reverse position from butt-joined, with the point of the rafter extending down (left, bottom). Rafter length must be measured from the topmost corner, even though this is not the farthest extending point of the rafter.

*Pole rafters, lightly hewed on top to give nailing surface, lapped and pegged. The temporary bracing was removed when the roof was boarded.*

The birdsmouth is a method of joining rafters to the plate unique to log-and-timber-frame construction. The joinery is named after the beak-like protrusion that enters the plate.

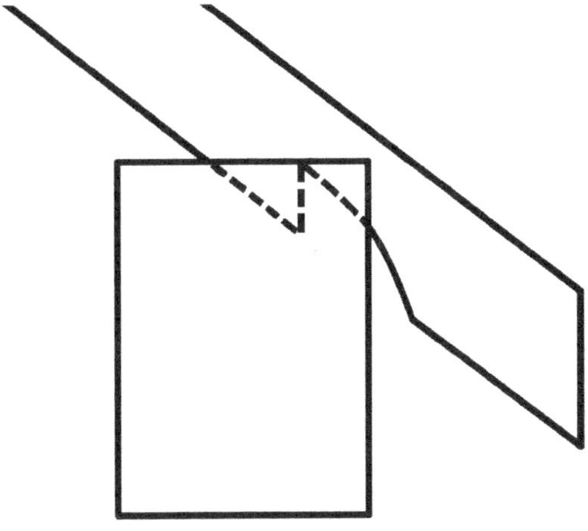

*Birdsmouth joint, showing how rafter penetrates and is secured by plate.*

If someone has concerns about his or her ability to cut complex joinery, they will surely have overcome those doubts by the time they have finished cutting these. With rafters two foot on center, even a modest cabin eighteen feet long will require twenty of these, and if the roof has a substantial overhang over the gables, another four will be required. The joint, however, is fairly forgiving. Errors that do not affect the height in which the rafter sits upon the plate will be easily absorbed and go virtually unnoticed. For those not wishing to engage in cutting this joint, the timbers can be cut as in conventional stud construction and either nailed or pegged. For the truly unskilled, skip joinery altogether. Put up a ridgepole, spike the rafter to the ridgepole and simply spike the rafter wherever it meets the plate. Call it good and ignore the following instructions on cutting a birdsmouth joint.

Since the rafter intersects the plate at the same angle as the roof pitch, the framing square is used to layout the birdsmouth onto the rafter as was used to cut the rafter peak.

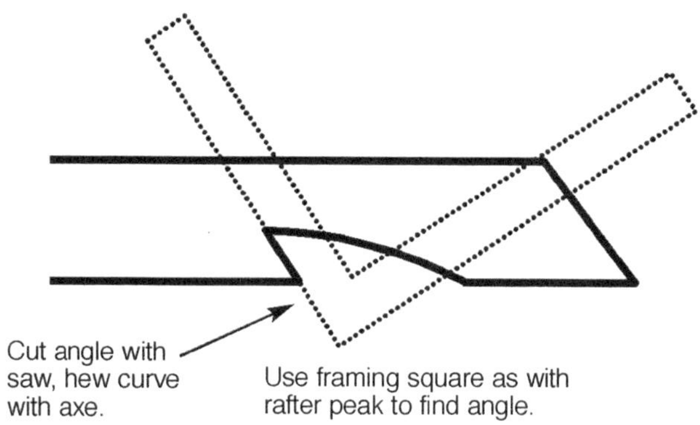


The vertical line is cut with either a handsaw or chain saw; the horizontal curve is hewn with axe or adze (see top photo on next page).

With the rafter completed, the plate must be notched to match the rafter. To do so I use a sliding bevel. One arm of the bevel is laid against the saw cut while the other arm rides along the rafter. Once properly fitted, the bevel's position is locked and the bevel is used as a guide while mortising the plate (see diagram at right).

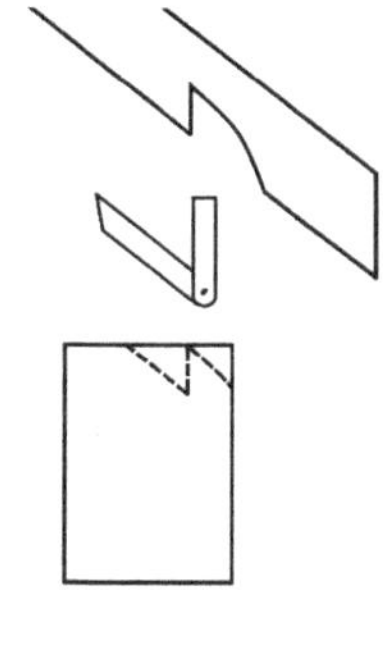

Now comes the chisel work. The back cut must be perfectly level, and the slope must match the sliding bevel. Chisel in straight along the back and side lines, then chisel out the waste.

*Curve of Birdsmouth hewn clean with axe.*

*Chisel out a pocket that is a mirror image of the rafter's birdsmouth.*

*Check with bevel to make certain mortise matches rafter.*

*Cutting backside of mortise with handsaw, using sliding bevel as saw guide.*

The back portion of the joint is easier to cut. To cut the backside, I hold the body of the sliding bevel against the mortise I had just chiseled and by eye, saw, attempting to match the sliding bevel's arm. Once the two saw cuts are completed, the waste between the saw cuts is chiseled out and the joint is finished.

I give the joint a trial fitting to see if either the rafter or plate need any further trimming.

*Trial fitting shows how the rafter fits into the Birdsmouth joint.*

I generally notch the rafter a full two inches. Two inches gives a good hold without weakening the rafter. If the rafter is less than six inches deep, I would notch the rafter less than two inches. You want to make sure you are notching the rafter to a depth of 1/3 its thickness or less.

Perhaps you find this roof framing dull and unchallenging. Perhaps you want the roof framing to be a statement of your ability as a craftsman and want this to stand out as the structure's most notable feature. Then take it another step and do as my brother Den did. He used large principle rafters spaced eight feet apart. The rafters are mortised, tenoned and pegged together. They are fitted to the plates with birdsmouth joinery. Space for a ridge beam was notched out at the peak and a ridge beam was hewn to match the roof pitch and fitted. Purlin pockets were chiseled out of the rafters every two feet. Purlins, hewn flat on the top surface, were fitted into the pockets using a foot adze. Hewn crossties were fitted into the notches and pegged. The whole roof structure was fitted onto knee walls, giving a complete open appearance to the second floor.

*Den places a spruce bough on the peak of his new hewn frame. Here is a roof structure to accentuate any hewn cabin or timber frame.*

As stated earlier in this work, if one wants to build a hewn log cabin or frame, it can be done. A hewing axe, a good saw and a few hand tools are all that are needed. Pick up the axe and discover the joy that comes from creating a structure out of nothing more than logs and one's own effort.

# THE FINAL STANCE

*I made no haste in my work, but rather the most of it . . .*
—Henry David Thoreau, *Walden.*

I have talked a great deal about stance. There is the stance for splitting wood, the stance for felling trees, the stance for hewing, scoring, etc. There is, however, one stance of which I have not spoken, and, if one is truly to enjoy axe work, it is the most important.

When Den and I first took to the woods with axes, we were young and driven. We would work long, hard, energetic hours with the axes, taking few breaks. While scoring and hewing, our hands would cramp up and we would have to peel our fingers from the axe handle.

Twenty-five years of axe work has brought about a change in attitude. I have no great burning desire to accomplish miracles in the woods. I do not feel pressured to hew so many beams per day. Hewing is my hobby, my recreation. It is as much an excuse to get out in the fresh air, in the woods and do some physical exercise. Axe work is physically demanding, but a joy if one learns the fine art of pacing oneself.

We live in a world that is obsessed with busy-ness. People barely know how to enjoy the moment. We are trying to accomplish something even if that something is just compulsively sending electronic messages back and forth. The axe breaks that compulsion.

When I work with axes, I score a little, then I sit on the log for a while. I score a little more and sit a little more. When I hew I do the same. The sitting is as much a part of the process as is the hewing. I do not sit because I am out of breath or exhausted. I sit because it is as much a part of the enjoyment as is the hewing. The work of scoring and hewing is physically demanding, and it was muscle fatigue that taught me to sit. But now that I have learned, I do it well before fatigue sets in.

Sitting is its own art. One can delight in the work that one has accomplished, but there are even more tantalizing distractions that await the quiet sitter. Two deer wandered by me once. A porcupine leading her baby tromped on through. Once as I sat, I looked into a tree to find that another was quietly watching me, an owl that finally took off with an almost silent flight. The forest air is also full of sounds, winter or summer. Depending upon the season, there are birds singing, frogs peeping, the siren of cicadas, or simply a vagrant wind meandering through the pines. In spring or fall there is the bug-less comfort of the pine-needle-covered forest floor. I cannot tell you how many times the outdoor air and pine-needle bed have led to a restful period of sleep.

Use the axe to break the chronic cycle of endless busy-ness. Take the time to enjoy the moment. Establish a natural rhythm with one's body, the wind, trees and earth. Swinging an axe is a primordial activity that awakens within the body just how natural and simple it is to feel alive.

# Endnotes

[1] Scoring is the process of chopping vertical stashes into the fallen tree. These slashes can be chopped by eye, or the scorer can follow a chalkline. What is important is that the scoring cuts follow a uniform depth so that when these scoring slashes are hewn off, the resulting surface is flat, true, and relatively smooth.

[2] C. Keith Wilbur, *Homebuilding and Woodworking in Colonial America,* The Globe Pequot Press, Old Saybrook, CT, 1992, pp. 5, 105.

[3] Funk and Wagnalls *Standard Desk Dictionary*, 1983.

[4] Raymond R. Townsend, "The Bearded Axe," *Fine Tool Journal,* Vol. 41, No. 2, Summer 1991, pp. 49-51.

[5] Bradford Angier, *How to Build Your Home in the Woods*, Hart Publishing Company, Inc., New York, 1952, p. 288 and p. 12.

[6] Funk and Wagnall's *New Encyclopedia,* 1972.

[7] Emily Weaver, *A Canadian History for Boys and Girls,* The Copp Clark Co., Toronto, 1919, p. 153. Donald Hutslar, *Log Construction in the Ohio Coun - try: 1750-1850*, Ohio Press University, Athens, 1992, p. 104.

[8] Charles M. Walker, *History of Athens County, Ohio*, Robert Clarke & Co., Cincinatti, 1869, pp. 115-116.

[9] John Langdon Sibley, *A History of the Town of Union,* New England History Press, Sommersworth, 1987, p. 98.

[10] *Ibid,* p. 98.

[11] Allen Goodwin Papers, Special Collections, Fogler Library, University of Maine, Orono.

[12] Frederick Jackson Turner, "The Significance of the Frontier in American History," Richard W. Etulain, *Does the Frontier Experience Make America Exceptional,* 1999, p. 29. Turner quoted from John Peck's *New Guide to the West,* Boston, 1837.

[13] *Ibid,* p. 29.

[14] Sibley, *Union*, for chronological account of early settlement, pp. 36-72.

[15] Henry David Thoreau, "Ktaadn," *The Maine Woods*, Penguin Books, New York, 1988, p. 24.

[16] *Ibid,* p. 23.

[17] *Ibid,* p. 32.

[18] Daniel C. Beard, *Shelters, Shacks and Shanties*, Shelter Publications, Bolinas, 1992, p. 212.

[19] Frank White, "Wood Fires and Firewood," *The Chronicle of the Early Ameri - can Industries Association*, Vol. 54, Number 1, March 2001, pp 26-30.

[20] David Havens, *The Wood Burners Handbook,* Harpswell Press, Brunswick, ME, 1973, p. 18.

[21] Stewart Brand, *The Next Whole Earth Catalog,* Point, 1980, p. 210.

[22] Bruce E. Cutter, "Preparing Wood for Your Wood Stove," University Extension, University of Missouri-Columbia, 1996.

[23] Ole Wik, *Wood Stoves: How to Make Them and Use Them,* Alaska Northwest Publishing, Anchorage, 1977, pp. 78-79.

[24] Lee Valley Tools, Ltd. and Veritas Tools Inc., >http://www.leevalley.com. 2000.

# BIBLIOGRAPHY

Angier, Bradford. *How to Build Your Home in the Woods*. Hart Publishing, Co.: New York. 1952.

Archives of Ontario.

Bailey, Francis, F. R. S. *Journal Tour in Unsettled Parts of North America in 1796 and 1797*, Bailey Brothers, London, Evans Microprint.

Beard, D. C. *Shelters, Shacks and Shanties.* Shelter Publications, Inc.: Bolinas, CA. 1992

Berg, Donald J., ed. *Homestead Hints.* Ten Speed Press: Berkeley, CA. 1986.

Brand, Stewart, ed. *The Next Whole Earth Catalog.* Point. 1980.

Broad-Axe Beam Co. "Hand-Hewn Beams." >>http://www.broadaxebeam.com. 2001.

Brown, Nelson; Moon, Franklin. *Elements of Forestry.* John Wiley & Sons, Inc.: New York. 1937.

Burkett, Charles William; Stevens, Frank Lincoln; Hill, Daniel Harvey. *Agriculture for Beginners.* Ginn and Company: Boston. 1914.

Cannie, Craig. "Hand Hewn: Woodcraft and Folk Ways Come Together in Peter Gott's Log Houses." *Harrowsmith.* July/August. 1988. pages 46-57.

Collins Axes >>http://www.mannedge.com/collins.htm. 2001.

Cumberland General Store *Wish and Want Book.*

Cutter, Bruce E. "Preparing Wood for Your Wood Stove." University Extension, University of Missouri-Columbia. 1996.

Dieter Schmidt Feine Werkzeuge >>http://www.fine-tools.com. 2001.

Fantasy Cutlery. "Viking Bearded Axe." >>http://www.fantasycutlery.com. 2001.

*Funk and Wagnall's New Encyclopedia.* 1972.

Goodwin Papers. Special Collections, Fogler Library. University of Maine: Orono.

Gransfors Bruks >>http://www.gransfors.com. 2001.

Havens, David. *The Woodburners Handbook.* Harpswell Press: Brunswick, ME. 1973.

Hunt, Clyde and Lancaster, Ken. "Improve Your Woodlot by Cutting Firewood." U.S.D.A. Forest Service, Northeastern Area State and Private Forestry. Broomall, PA.

Hustlar, Donald A. *Log Construction in the Ohio Country: 1750-1850.* Ohio Press University: Athens. 1992.

Kahn, Loydd. *Shelter.* Shelter Publications: Bolinas, CA. 1971.

Langsner, Drew. *A Logbuilders Handbook.* Rodale Press: Emmaus, PA. 1982.

Lee Valley Tools, Ltd. and Veritas Tools, Inc. >>http://www.leevalley.com. 2001.

Lehman's General Store >>http://www.lehmans.com. 2001.

Library of Congress.

Manning, Samuel. *New England Masts and the King's Broad Arrow.* Tilbury House Publishers: Gardiner, ME. 1979.

National Archives of Canada.

Northdoorway Homestead Outfitters >>http://northdoorway.com/farmgarden/fellingaxe.htm. 2001.

Ridlon, G. T., Sr. *Saco Valley Settlements And Families.* Published by the Author: Portland. 1895

Schroeder's Log Home Supply >>http://www.loghelp.com. 2001.

Sibley, John Langsdon. *A History of the Town of Union.* New England History Press: Sommersworth. 1987.

Snow and Nealley. "Axes and Mauls." >>http://www.snowandnealley.com. 2001.

*The Western Miscellany.* Dayton. Vol. 1, July1848. Page 342.

Thoreau, Henry David. "Ktaadn." *The Maine Woods.* Penguin Books: New York. 1988.

Thoreau, Henry David. *Walden & The Essay on Civil Disobedience.* Lancer Books: New York. 1968.

Townsend, Raymond R. "The Bearded Axe." *Fine Tool Journal.* Vol. 41. No. 2. Summer 1991.

Turner, Frederick Jackson. "The Significance of the Frontier in American History." Etulain, Richard W., ed. *Does the Frontier Experience Make America Exceptional.* 1999.

Walker, Charles M. *History of Athens County, Ohio.* Robert Clarke & Company: Cincinatti. 1869.

Weaver, Emily. *A Canadian History for Boys and Girls.* The Copp Clark Company, Limited: Toronto. 1919.

Williams, John S., ed. "Our Cabin; or, Life in the Woods." *American Pioneer* 2, no. 10, October 1843. Pages 453-459.

White, Frank G. "Wood Fires and Firewood." *The Chronicle of the Early American Industries Association.* Vol. 54, No. 1. March 2001.

Wik, Ole. *Wood Stoves: How to Make Them and Use Them.* Alaska Northwest Publishing: Anchorage. 1977.

Woodcraft Supply >>http://www.woodcraft.com. 2001.

Woodings-Verona >>http://www.woodings-verona. 2001.

# FURTHER READING

Angier, Bradford and Whelen, Townsend. *On Your Own in the Wilderness.* The Stackpole Company: Harrisburg, PA. 1958.

Bealer, Alex W. *Old Ways of Working Wood.* Barre Publishing: Barre, MA. 1972.

Bealer, Alex W. and Ellis, John O. *The Log Cabin: Homes of the American Wilderness.* Barre Publishing: Barre, MA.

Beaudry, Michael. "Mudpond Hewing." >>http://www.mudpond.net. 2001.

Bruyere, Christian and Inwood, Robert. *In Harmony with Nature.* Drake Publishers: New York. 1975.

Cook. *Keeping Warm with an Ax.* Universe Books: New York. 1981.

Elliot, Stewart and Wallas, Eugene. *The Timber Framing Book.* Housesmith Press: York, ME. 1977.

Foster, David R. and O'Keefe, John F. *New England Forests Through Time: Insights from the Harvard Forest Dioramas.* Harvard Forest: Petersham, MA. Harvard University. 2000.

Greear, Delbert. "Making Ax Handles." *Fine Woodworking on Hand Tools.* The Taunton Press: Newton, CT. 1986.

Gregory, Mark. "Basic Axemanship." *The Mother Earth News Handbook of Homemade Power.* Bantam Books: New York. 1974.

Heavrin, Charles A. *The Axe and Man.* The Astragal Press: Mendham, NJ. 1998.

Honer, T. G. "Shantyman Forest Heritage Cards, Celebrating Canada's Square Timber Trade." >>http://www. shanty mannart.com/heritage.html.

Klenman, Allen. *Axe Makers of North America.* Curries Forest-graphics, Ltd.: Victoria, B.C. 1990.

Langsner, Drew. *Country Woodcraft.* Rodale Press: Emmaus, PA. 1978.

Langsner, Drew. "Hewing" and "Cleaving Wood." *Fine Wood - working On Hand Tools.* The Taunton Press: Newton, CT. 1986.

McRaven, Charles. *Building and Restoring the Hewn Log House.* Betterway Books: Cincinatti, OH. 1994.

*Muir's Original Log Home Guide.* Annual 1993 Directory.

*Muir's Original Log Home Guide.* Log Structures Restoration Guide.

Nearing, Helen and Scott. *Continuing the Good Life.* Schocken Books: New York. 1979.

Nearing, Helen and Scott. *The Maple Sugar Book.* Schocken Books: New York. 1950.

Pomerleau, Jeanne. *Bucherons, Raftmen et Draveurs 1850-1960.* J. C. Dupont: Sainte Foy, Quebec. 1997.

Sloane, Eric. *Sketches of America Past.* Promontory Press: New York. 1986.

Smith, David. "A Life in the Woods." *A History of Lumbering in Maine: 1860-1960.* University of Maine: Orono, ME. 1972.

Tresemer, David. *Splitting Firewood.* Hand and Foot, Ltd.: Brattleboro, VT. 1981.

Underhill, Roy. *The Woodwright's Electric Workshop.* The University of North Carolina Press: Chapel Hill. 1991.

Underhill, Roy. *The Woodwright's Shop.* The University of North Carolina Press: Chapel Hill. 1981.

Wigginton, Elliot, ed. *The Foxfire Book.* Anchor Press: Garden City, NY. 1972.

Wilbur, Keith C. *Homebuilding and Woodworking in Colonial America.* The Globe Pequot Press: Old Saybrook, CT. 1992.

Wilder, Laura Ingalls. *Little House on the Prairie.* Harper Collins: New York. 1971.

# INDEX

## About the Author

Mike Beaudry received his B. S. in Education from the University of Maine. With his wife, Claudette, and two children, Jesse and Emma, he has homesteaded, farmed and raised animals in Maine for 25 years. His articles have appeared in *Countryside and Small Stock Journal* and *The Bangor Daily,* and he has lectured at historical societies and museums. His hewn timbers have appeared in several structures, barns and houses in the area, and his hewing abilities have caught the attention of historical preservationists. He frequently does hewing and shake splitting demonstrations at museums, living history centers, and selected fairs. In addition, he teaches hand hewing at his Montville home.

Mike is also a historian engaged in researching log construction in New England. He has traveled extensively in the Northeast, including the Canadian Maritimes and parts of Quebec, researching and photographing log structures. He has studied the 17th century "Logg" garrison houses of coastal Maine and New Hampshire, the Acadien and Quebecois piece sur piece log homes of Northern Maine and Vermont, the scribed fit hewn log homes of the 19th century Swedish immigrants, sporting and lumber camps, and the log forts and blockhouses of predominantly 18th century northern New England.

His interest has led him to study not only the way the logs were joined but to study the axemanship involved in shaping the timbers. He believes the tool marks on old timbers can be read, telling us not only of the axeman's skill, but of his haste or patience, and about the axe used. Mike believes this is essential in doing restoration work. The craftsman must be able to recreate any hewn surface, whether rough or smooth, left by the original builder.

He has conversed with preservationists, historians, log builders, timber framers, hewers, and shingle splitters, gleaning from each ideas that have helped refine his own techniques.

Mike is currently undertaking the construction of a hewn double pen barn.